Microwave Cooking

BY BARBARA WASSER

GROSSET
GOOD LIFE
BOOKS

Publishers · GROSSET & DUNLAP · New York
A FILMWAYS COMPANY

ACKNOWLEDGMENTS

Cover photograph by Mort Engel

Text photographs by Clarence Nevis, excepting those otherwise credited.

I am indebted to Shirlee Smith and Nancy Kostman for their help in testing recipes; to Corning Glass Works for Pyrex and Corning Ware; to numerous appliance dealers for the use of microwave ovens; and to my many friends, my husband and my children who enjoyed the "tests."

Many of the recipes in this book first appeared in *Cooking with Microwaves* © 1974 by Barbara Wasser.

Instructions for recipes and safety precautions in this book have been carefully checked for accuracy. However, the author and publisher do not warrant or guarantee results and cannot be responsible for any adverse consequences resulting from the use of information contained herein. The author has attempted to assist the reader in avoiding problems by setting forth appropriate and recommended procedures.

Contents

1
Using Your Microwave Oven

Microwave cooking fits right into our modern life-style. It is fast, exciting, and convenient. And since the microwave oven uses only half the energy of a conventional range, it also saves money and conserves energy. It is not surprising that the microwave oven is fast becoming a necessary and often used appliance in every home.

This book was written to help you take advantage of this fantastic new cooking method, and expand your use of it beyond the basic recipes given in your oven manufacturer's instruction booklets. Every one of the dishes described and pictured here was prepared in a portable or counter-top microwave oven. By following these tested recipes, you can transform the everyday task of cooking into an exciting adventure—the quick and easy microwave way!

Understanding Microwave Cooking

Microwave energy is radiant energy. A form of very-high-frequency radio waves is generated by an electron tube (magnetron) inside the oven. These microwaves, when released inside the oven, bounce off the metal of the oven cavity. They penetrate food placed in the oven, and make the food molecules vibrate at a fantastic rate. The friction caused by this vibration creates heat within the food, cooking it rapidly. The process is like creating heat by rubbing your hands together fast.

Since heat is generated within the food, your oven and your kitchen stay cool. Foods don't bake onto a cool surface, so you have a cleaner oven.

Microwave ovens have a variety of built-in safety devices, such as indicator lights and separate interlock door switches, to insure that the user will never come in contact with the microwaves. Even though the only possible harm microwave energy can cause is a skin burn, the oven automatically shuts off whenever the door is opened.

Different ovens vary in cooking time; power output varies from 450 watts to 700 watts. The recipes in this book are based on an average wattage of 600 to 650. If your oven has more or less than the average wattage, it will be necessary to adjust the cooking time.

If 1 cup of water boils in 2½ to 3 minutes in your oven, you should have no trouble with the times in this cookbook.

The Tappan Company

The number of minutes given at the top of each recipe is the total oven time. To "turn" the baking dish means to switch front and back, or turn it around 180°.

Use and Care of Your Oven

Always operate the oven according to manufacturer's instructions.

Do not try to defeat safety mechanisms like the door interlocks.

Keep the oven clean, especially around the door seals; clean with a damp, soapy cloth.

If the door interlock fails for any reason, do not use the oven until it has been repaired by a competent serviceman.

To insure proper cooking, use the correct sizes of house wiring and fuses as directed by manufacturer.

Do not use a meat or candy thermometer in the oven when it is operating. Use only after the food is removed from the oven. Special thermometers designed for microwave use are available; check your dealer for information.

Cooking Utensils

Microwaves are absorbed, reflected, or trans-

ferred. Cooking utensils should be selected according to their reaction to the microwaves. Most foods should be cooked in a utensil that transfers the energy to the food being cooked.

Do not use metal cooking utensils in the oven. Metal reflects the microwaves and prevents them from reaching the food inside the container. Some manufacturers recommend the occasional use of small pieces of metal and even containers like TV trays, but they should be used in your oven only if the manufacturer's instructions state that they can be.

Do not use any dish that has a metal trim of any type—such as gold or silver. Check the underside of any dish to be sure there is no metal on the signature.

Glass and China

Glass, glass ceramic, and pottery can all be used in a microwave oven. Microwaves pass through glass, so it is excellent for use in the oven.

However, some glass may have a paint or glaze that contains a metallic substance, and should not be used. To test glassware that you have any doubts about, place it in the oven and turn the oven on for 20 to 30 seconds. If the glassware has not become warm or hot, it is all

Glass-ceramic pottery and glass cooking utensils

Plastic and plastic foam cooking utensils

right to use in the oven.

Corning ware, Pyrex, Corelle, Creative glass, Glassbake, oven-proof baking dishes, plates, serving dishes, storage jars, glass measuring cups, canning jars, and cups can all be used.

But *do not* use Corning Centura dinnerware or Corelle Livingware closed-handle cups. They contain a glaze that attracts microwaves.

Note: The 1½-quart utility dish referred to in some recipes as being 7 x 11 inches in size actually measures 7½ x 11¾. It may be called an 8 x 12 dish in some of your oven manufacturers' cookbooks.

Paper and Plastic

Paper products transfer microwaves and are used mainly when foods are being heated. They include napkins, towels, plates, containers for frozen foods or take-out foods, and freezer wrap.

Plastics that are dishwasher safe can be used in the microwave oven. Plastic foam cups and bowls are good for heating foods and liquids. Plastic bags and pouches should be used only if they are specially designed for cooking.

Republic Freezette plastic containers come in many shapes and sizes that are good for use in the microwave oven.

Paper towels or napkins can be used to avoid splattering or to absorb moisture when heating bread products.

Plastic wrap is used to cover dishes that have no cover or for a tighter seal than wax paper. Be careful when removing as it holds steam.

Wood and Straw

Wooden trays or utensils are not recommended for cooking in the microwave. Wooden spoons or wooden-handled spatulas become warm but are not damaged.

Straw baskets are only used for a short time, as for heating bread or rolls.

Browning Dishes

Browning dishes are glass-ceramic dishes with a special coating applied to the outside bottom of the dish. When the empty dish is preheated in the microwave oven, the special coating interacts with microwave energy and produces heat.

Microwave browning dishes have feet to raise the dish above the microwave oven shelf. This prevents the oven shelf from absorbing heat from the dish and getting hot enough to cause possible breakage.

A microwave browning dish is specially coated and has feet.

Wooden or straw cooking utensils

2
Appetizers

Hot appetizers can be served on toothpicks or as canapes, dips, or fondue. Most of them can be prepared ahead and stored in the refrigerator or freezer, then heated in the microwave oven just before serving. Arrange appetizers on a paper plate with an attractive doily, using a pan liner or paper toweling under the doily for very moist foods. Keep portions the same size so none will over-cook, and cover with plastic or foil wrap. (Foil must be removed before heating; plastic can be left on.) Most appetizers take 20 to 25 seconds to heat up; frozen ones take about 45 seconds.

Cheese and cracker canapes can be made more interesting by topping them with bits of crisp bacon, toasted nuts, dried beef strips, anchovies, tiny canned shrimps, or flaked tuna or crab meat. Moist canapes can be decorated with olive or green pepper slices, parsley, chives, or red onion strips. Toothpick hors d'oeuvres can combine tiny weiners or shrimps with chunks of pineapple, olives or sardines wrapped in strips of boiled ham, cheese hunks wrapped in dried beef, or tiny pickled onions and sweet gherkins with maraschino cherries.

Next time you give a party, try setting out dishes of hors d'oeuvres, each marked with cooking time, and let each guest have the fun of warming up a paper plateful.

Pineapple Bacon Rolls
4 to 5 minutes

1 can pineapple chunks, drained
½ lb. bacon, sliced thin

Wrap each pineapple chunk with ⅓ slice of bacon. Secure with wooden toothpick. Place 12 in a circle on 3 or 4 thicknesses of paper toweling on paper or china plate. Cover with another paper towel. Cook until bacon is brown and crisp, 4 to 5 minutes.
Makes 24 to 30.

Rumakis

3½ to 4 minutes

1 (6 oz.) can water chestnuts, drained	½ cup soy sauce
	¼ tsp. ginger
½ lb. chicken livers	¼ tsp. curry powder
½ lb. bacon slices, cut in half	

Cut water chestnuts and chicken livers into thirds, and fold liver over water chestnut. Wrap a strip of bacon around them and secure with a toothpick. Marinate 15 minutes in soy sauce, ginger, and curry powder. Arrange on a double layer of paper toweling laid on a paper plate. Cover with another paper towel. Cook 3½ to 4 minutes. Serve hot.

Makes 24 to 30.

Cheese Canapés

45 seconds to 1 minute

2 cups shredded sharp cheddar cheese	3 Tbs. chili sauce
	36 melba toast rounds or other crackers
⅓ cup imitation bacon bits	
1 medium onion; minced fine	

Mix cheese, bacon bits, onion, and chili sauce thoroughly. Spread on toast rounds. Place 12 on serving dish or paper plate. Heat 45 seconds to 1 minute. Serve hot.

Makes 36.

Mini Pizzas

¾ to 1 minute

1 package (4 oz.) pepperoni slices	1 can (6 oz.) tomato paste
1 package (6 oz.) mozzarella cheese slices	Oregano
	Melba toast rounds

Spread tomato paste on toast rounds. Top with pepperoni slice and cheese slice, sprinkle top with oregano. Place 12 on paper plate or serving dish. Heat 45 seconds to 1 minute. Serve hot.

Makes 36.

From back to front, Pineapple Bacon Rolls, Cheese Canapés, Meatballs, and Mini Pizza appetizers

Saucy Sausages

Meatballs
5 to 8 minutes

1 lb. ground round beef	½ cup bread crumbs
2 Tbs. onion soup mix	½ cup tomato juice
1 tsp. salt	
2 Tbs. Worcestershire sauce	

Mix ingredients together. Form into 20 1-inch balls. Place on meat platter or in utility dish. Cook 5 to 8 minutes, turning meatballs after half the cooking time. Serve with your favorite sauce.

Makes 20.

Saucy Sausages
4 to 5 minutes

2 (5 oz.) packages tiny smoked sausages, precooked	½ cup currant or grape jelly
	½ cup chili sauce
1 (13½ oz.) can pineapple tidbits, drained	1½ Tbs. lemon juice
	1½ Tbs. prepared mustard

Cut each sausage in half diagonally lengthwise. With toothpick, fasten a pineapple tidbit to cut side of each sausage half.

Combine jelly, chili sauce, lemon juice, and mustard in a 7 x 11-inch (1½-quart) baking dish. Arrange sausages in sauce. Cover with wax paper or plastic wrap. Cook 4 to 5 minutes. Serve hot.

Makes 64.

Hot Stuffed Mushrooms
7¼ to 9⅓ minutes

¼ cup butter or margarine	½ cup grated Parmesan cheese
24 small whole fresh mushrooms, stems removed	¼ cup sliced almonds
1 (3 oz.) package softened cream cheese	

Melt butter (15–20 seconds) in 7 x 11-inch (1½-quart) utility dish. Add mushroom caps; shake until all caps are covered with butter. Cook 4 to 5 minutes.

Combine cream cheese and Parmesan cheese. Spoon mixture into cavity of each mushroom cap; stick 3 or 4 almond slices into each cheese filling. Heat thoroughly, 3 to 4 minutes. Serve at once.

Makes 24.

Dips and Fondues

By scooping up a dab of delicious dip or coating a munchy morsel with a rich or tangy fondue, your guests take an active part in pleasing their own palates. Here are some popular dishes to have on hand at your next affair.

Hot Clam Dip
6 to 7 minutes

1 (7 oz.) can minced clams	2 Tbs. chopped ripe olives
2 Tbs. minced onion	1 Tbs. catsup
2 Tbs. butter or margarine	1 tsp. Worcestershire sauce
1 cup grated sharp cheese	Few drops Tabasco
	Crackers or chips

Drain clams, reserving 1 tablespoon of the liquid. In mixing bowl, combine onion and butter. Cook 3 minutes. Add clams, reserved clam liquid, cheese, chopped olives, and seasonings. Heat until cheese is melted, 3 to 4 minutes, stirring after 1 minute. Serve with crackers or chips.

Makes 1¼ cups.

Pizza Fondue
10 to 12 minutes

1 onion, chopped	¼ tsp. garlic powder
1 stalk celery, chopped	2 (10½ oz.) cans pizza sauce
½ lb. ground beef	2 Tbs. grated Parmesan cheese
2 Tbs. salad oil	
1 Tbs. cornstarch	
1½ tsp. oregano	

1½ cups grated cheddar cheese	French bread, cubed and toasted
1 cup grated mozzarella cheese	

Brown onion, celery, and ground beef in salad oil in 2-quart casserole dish, 4 to 5 minutes. Mix cornstarch and seasonings into pizza sauce and add to meat. Stir well and cook 3 to 4 minutes. When mixture is thickened and bubbling, add cheese by thirds, cooking about 1 minute after each addition. Stir well after each addition. When cheese is melted and hot, serve with toasted bread cubes.

Reheat if necessary, or transfer to fondue pot or chafing dish.

Makes 1 quart.

Chili con Queso
9 to 11 minutes

1 medium onion, chopped	1 (4 oz.) can diced chilies
1 small green pepper, chopped	1 lb. sharp cheese, grated
1 Tbs. salad oil	1 tsp. seasoned salt
5 fresh medium tomatoes, chopped, or 5 whole, well-drained canned tomatoes	½ tsp. monosodium glutamate (optional)
	Salt and pepper to taste

Combine onion, green pepper, and salad oil in 1½-quart casserole. Cook 5 to 6 minutes. Stir in tomatoes, chilies, cheese, and seasonings. Stir well. Cook 4 to 5 minutes, stirring after 2 minutes.

Serve with corn or tortilla chips, returning to oven and reheating for a few minutes if necessary.

Makes 4 cups.

Chocolate Mint Fondue
1½ to 2½ minutes

1 (12 oz.) package semisweet chocolate pieces	⅔ cup chocolate-mint liqueur or 2 tsp. mint extract
½ pt. (1 cup) dairy sour cream	

Chocolate Mint Fondue

Melt chocolate in a 2-quart casserole, 1½ to 2½ minutes. Stir in sour cream and liqueur. Continue stirring until mixture is well blended. Serve with banana chunks, strawberries, marshmallows, maraschino cherries, cubes of angel or pound cake, or pretzel sticks. Fondue will stay at dipping consistency for about 1 hour.

Serves 8 to 12.

Fondue José
3 to 4 minutes

- 1 tsp. oregano leaves
- 2 cups (8 oz.) shredded cheddar cheese
- 2 cans (15½ oz.) Sloppy Joe mix with meat

Combine all ingredients in a 2½ to 3-quart casserole. Cook 3 to 4 minutes, stirring occasionally. Serve hot with bread cubes or tortilla or taco chips.

Makes 8 to 10 servings.

Corn and Frank Chowder

3
Soups and Sandwiches

Soups

One of the new colored casserole dishes is just as pretty on the table as a tureen for soups. Or how about a bean pot? In fact, you can use any heat-proof bowl without a metal trim.

Divide canned soups into individual soup dishes, dilute, and heat. No pot to wash.

Soups containing milk boil over quickly and must be watched during cooking. Use a container twice as deep as the ingredients. Stir soup whenever it starts to boil.

Mix and match soups to create a specialty of your own. Dilute with water or milk, then add meat, seafood, vegetables, or pasta for a hearty meal.

Garnish soups with chopped parsley or chives, crumbled cooked bacon or bacon bits, grated cheese, lemon slices, paprika, sliced olives, sour cream, plain or garlic croutons, slivered salted almonds or cashews, crisp ready-to-eat cereal, and that old favorite, crisp crackers.

Corn and Frank Chowder
20½ to 24 minutes

3 slices bacon, chopped	2 tsp. salt
5 frankfurters, sliced	¼ tsp. pepper
1 medium onion, chopped	½ tsp. basil
4 medium potatoes, diced	1 (1 lb.) can cream-style corn
1 cup water	1 (15½ oz.) can evaporated milk

Place bacon in 2½ quart casserole. Cook 2½ to 3 minutes. Add franks and onion. Cook 4 minutes, stirring after 2 minutes. Add potatoes and water. Cover and cook 10 to 12 minutes, turning dish halfway through cooking. Add remaining ingredients and heat to serving temperature, 4 to 5 minutes, do not boil.

Serves 6.

Clam Chowder
18 to 23 minutes

2 slices bacon, diced
1 medium onion, chopped
2 (7½ oz.) cans chopped clams
3 cups water
3 medium potatoes, cubed
3 Tbs. flour
2 Tbs. butter or margarine
2 cups milk (part cream)
3 tsp. salt
¼ tsp. pepper

Cook bacon and onion in 3-quart casserole dish 4 to 5 minutes, stirring twice. Drain clams and combine the liquid with 2 cups of the water in dish with bacon and onions. Add potatoes; cover and cook 10 to 12 minutes, stirring after half of the cooking time. Blend flour with the remaining cup of water. Add to potatoes, stir well. Add all the remaining ingredients. Heat but do not boil, 4 to 6 minutes.
Serves 6.

Beanestrone
10 to 13 minutes

1 can (12 oz.) luncheon meat or 1 cup cooked ham, cubed
2 Tbs. chopped onion
1 Tbs. butter or margarine
1 can (11½ oz.) condensed bean with bacon soup
1 can (10¾ oz.) condensed minestrone soup
2 soup cans water

Combine meat, onion, and butter in 2-quart casserole dish. Cook, stirring once, 4 to 5 minutes. Stir in soups and water. Heat, stirring once, 6 to 8 minutes.
Serves 6.

Greek Lemon Soup
15 to 18 minutes

2 (10½ oz.) cans chicken broth
2 Tbs. raw rice
1 tsp. grated lemon peel
2 Tbs. lemon juice
1 egg, beaten
1 lemon, thinly sliced
Snipped parsley

Combine broth and rice in 3-quart covered

Greek Lemon Soup

casserole. Cook 10 to 12 minutes. Let stand covered 20 minutes. Combine lemon peel, lemon juice, and egg. Pour small amount of hot broth into egg mixture, stirring constantly. Return to hot broth. Heat in covered casserole, but do not boil, 5 to 6 minutes. Serve immediately in individual soup bowls, topped with slice of lemon and garnished with parsley.
Serves 4.

Hot Tomato Bouillon
5 to 7 minutes

1 (10½ oz.) can condensed tomato soup
1 (10½ oz.) can condensed beef broth
½ soup can water
⅛ tsp. crushed oregano
Dash of garlic powder
1 avocado, thinly sliced

Combine soups, water, and seasonings. Cook 5 to 7 minutes. Pour into soup tureen or soup dishes; float slices of avocado on top.
Serves 4.

Sandwiches

Combinations of ham, corned beef hash, bologna, bacon, or baked beans with cheese, tomato, relish, and seasonings make delicious closed or open-faced sandwiches. Heat sandwiches on a serving plate, paper towel, or paper plate, covered with a paper towel. Heat only until filling is warmed or cheese melts. Overcooking causes bread to lose moisture. Frozen sandwiches should be thawed before heating.

Be sure to cover buns with a paper towel or napkin or place in a paper bag. Heat only until slightly warm. They continue to get hotter after removing from oven. Sprinkle a little water on day-old or dried-out rolls, buns, or breads before heating.

Sloppy Joes

Deviled Ham Roundups
1½ to 2½ minutes

1 (2¼ oz.) can deviled ham	6 slices raw tomato
2 Tbs. mayonnaise	6 slices cheese
3 hamburger buns, split	

Mix ham with mayonnaise. Spread on half of bun. Top with tomato slice and slice of cheese. Cook in 7 x 11-inch glass baking dish 1½ to 2½ minutes.

Makes 6.

Chili con Carne con Frijoles
10 to 12 minutes

1 lb. ground beef	1 (1 lb.) can tomatoes
1 tsp. seasoned salt	4 hamburger buns
1 (1¼ oz.) package chili seasoning mix	1 cup grated cheese
¼ cup water	
1 (1 lb.) can kidney or pinto beans	

Brown meat in 2-quart casserole dish, breaking up until crumbly with a fork, 4 to 5 minutes. Add seasonings, water, beans, and tomatoes, stirring to blend. Cover and cook 6 to 7 minutes, stirring once. Serve on buns with grated cheese sprinkled over the meat mixture.

Buns can be warmed in the microwave first. Serves 4.

Sloppy Joes
34 to 36 minutes

2½ medium onions, chopped	¾ cup pickle relish
2 medium green peppers, chopped	1 tsp. dry mustard
1½ stalks celery, chopped	¼ tsp. garlic powder
3 lbs. ground round beef	1 tsp. salt
1½ cups catsup	½ tsp. pepper
1½ cans undiluted tomato soup	1 (8 oz.) can sliced mushrooms, drained
	12 hamburger buns

Combine onions, green peppers, and celery in 7 x 11-inch utility dish. Cook, stirring occasionally, 6 to 7 minutes. Add crumbled meat to vegetables and cook, stirring occasionally, 8 to 9 minutes. Pour vegetables and meat into 3-quart casserole dish. Add all remaining ingredients except mushrooms. Cover and cook 20 minutes, stirring every 5 minutes. Add mushrooms and serve over warmed hamburger buns or onion rolls.

For fewer servings, make whole recipe and store leftover filling in refrigerator or freezer.

Serves 12.

Stuffed Corned Beef Sandwich
5 to 7 minutes

12 frankfurter buns
1½ cups shredded corned beef
1½ cups chopped ripe olives
6 Tbs. minced green onion
3 Tbs. minced green pepper
¾ cup catsup
3 Tbs. Worcestershire sauce
Salt to taste

Split buns and scoop out soft centers. Combine remaining ingredients. Fill rolls and replace tops. Wrap each bun in a paper towel or napkin. Heat, 6 at a time, 2½ to 3½ minutes.

Sandwiches may be wrapped individually in plastic wrap or foil and frozen. Thaw before heating.

Makes 12.

Luncheon Shrimp
3 to 5 minutes

4 hamburger buns, halved, toasted lightly
1½ cups shredded cheddar cheese
4 hard-cooked eggs, chopped
2 cans (4½ oz.) shrimp
3 Tbs. celery, chopped
1½ Tbs. onion, minced
¼ tsp. garlic, minced
⅓ cup black olives, sliced
2 Tbs. mayonnaise
Salt to taste

Put hamburger buns in 7 x 11-inch utility dish. Set aside ½ cup cheese. Combine all ingredients. Use just enough mayonnaise to hold ingredients together. Spread on buns and top with remaining cheese. Cook until hot and cheese melts, 3 to 5 minutes. Serve on plate garnished with large green pepper ring filled with cherry tomatoes, carrot curls, or cucumber sticks.

Serves 8.

Tomato Crabmeat Sandwich
3 to 3½ minutes

1 (6½ oz.) can crabmeat
2 Tbs. mayonnaise
1 tsp. salt
¼ tsp. ground black pepper
6 French rolls, sliced in half lengthwise and toasted
12 slices tomato
Parsley

Luncheon Shrimp

Flake crabmeat and combine with mayonnaise, salt, and pepper. Spread on each toasted half of rolls. Top with tomato. Place in baking dish or platter. Heat 3 to 3½ minutes. Serve garnished with parsley.

You can substitute fresh crab or tiny shrimp, or add sliced cheese to top of sandwich. Allow extra heating time to melt cheese.

Makes 6.

Creamed Shrimp on Toast
6½ to 8½ minutes

2 cans (10½ oz.) cream of mushroom soup, not diluted	12 ripe olives, sliced
	¼ tsp. paprika
	Salt to taste
1 can (7 oz.) mushroom stems and pieces	8 slices pimiento cheese
2 cups cooked shrimp or 2 cans (4½ oz.) shrimp	8 slices bread, lightly toasted

Pour soup into 2-quart casserole dish. Stir; cook 1½ to 2 minutes. Add mushrooms, shrimp, olives, paprika, and salt. Cook 4 to 5 minutes. Place bread, 4 slices at a time, in 7 x 11-inch utility dish. Top with cheese. Cook until cheese melts, 1 to 1½ minutes. Spoon creamed shrimp over cheese toast.

Serves 8.

Tomato Crabmeat Sandwich

4
Salads

You can use your microwave oven in making salads that call for gelatin or cooked vegetables. In addition to your favorite hot salads, use it for cooked dressings too. Stir them with a wooden spoon that can be left in the oven.

Potato Salad
16 to 19 minutes

6 medium potatoes	1 Tbs. prepared mustard
6 hard-cooked eggs	1 Tbs. vinegar
½ to ¾ cup chopped	1½ tsp. salt
green or regular onion	1 tsp. sugar
¼ to ½ cup chopped celery	½ tsp. pepper
1 cup mayonnaise or salad dressing	Paprika

Bake potatoes in their jackets 16 to 19 minutes. Cook those of uniform size together. Arrange potatoes about an inch apart on a paper towel. Rotate them after half the cooking time. Prick each potato all the way through with a large fork or paring knife.

Cool potatoes slightly, peel and dice. Chop and add 5 eggs; slice and reserve one for garnish. Add onion and celery. Toss slightly. Combine remaining ingredients and fold into potato mixture. Garnish with egg slices. Sprinkle with paprika. Refrigerate several hours to let the flavors blend.

For variation, substitute one or a combination of the following:

¼ to ½ cup chopped sweet or dill pickle	¼ tsp. oregano leaves
	¼ tsp. savory leaves
1 to 2 tsp. celery seed	Lemon juice instead of vinegar
2 to 3 Tbs. minced parsley	1 to 2 tsp. chopped capers
2 to 4 Tbs. chopped green pepper	2 to 3 tsp. horseradish
¼ to ½ cup peeled chopped cucumber	1 to 2 Tbs. chopped pimiento
2 to 4 Tbs. chopped radish	½ to 1 cup cubed ham
⅛ tsp. garlic powder	¼ cup grated carrots
Serves 6 to 8.	

Hot Bean Slaw
3 to 5 minutes

1 (16 oz.) can diagonal cut green beans, drained	3 slices bacon
	2½ Tbs. vinegar
	1 Tbs. sugar
	1 tsp. salt
1 cup diced celery	Dash of pepper
2 Tbs. diced pimiento	Lettuce leaves

Toss beans with celery and pimiento in medium-size bowl; chill thoroughly. Cook bacon until crisp in a 7 x 11-inch baking dish, without using paper towels, 2 to 3 minutes.

Remove bacon; reserve drippings. Stir in vinegar, sugar, salt, and pepper. Heat 1 to 2 minutes to dissolve sugar and salt. Pour hot over bean mixture; toss lightly to coat. Spoon into lettuce-lined salad bowls; top with crumbled bacon. Serve at once.

Serves 4 to 6.

Spinach Salad
4 to 6 minutes

8 slices bacon	½ cup canned black-eyed peas, drained
2 bunches fresh spinach	
4 hard-cooked eggs, chopped	1 Tbs. grated onion

Lay bacon slices in paper-towel-lined 7 x 11-inch oblong dish. Cover with towel. Cook 4 to 6 minutes. Crumble and set aside. Tear spinach into bite-size pieces. In large salad bowl, combine bacon, spinach, cooked eggs, peas, and onion. Toss with dressing.

Dressing

¾ cup salad oil	½ tsp. dry mustard
½ cup wine vinegar	Freshly ground pepper
1 tsp. salt	

Combine ingredients and mix thoroughly. Bacon drippings may be substituted for part of the oil.

Serves 8.

Hot Turkey Salad
5 minutes

1 cup mayonnaise	½ cup sliced almonds
2 Tbs. lemon juice	
½ tsp. salt	2 to 4 hard-cooked eggs (optional)
2 Tbs. grated onion	
2 cups cooked turkey	½ cup grated cheese
2 cups chopped celery	1 cup crushed potato chips

Blend mayonnaise, lemon juice, salt, and grated onion together and mix lightly with

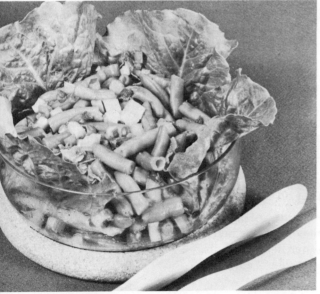

Hot Bean Slaw

Hot Turkey Salad

turkey, celery, almonds, and eggs. Pile lightly into greased 8 x 8 inch baking dish. Sprinkle grated cheese and potato chips on top. Cook 5 minutes.

Chicken, shrimp, or tuna may be substituted for the turkey.

Serves 4 to 6.

Hot Spiced Fruit Salad
7 minutes

2 (1 lb.) cans fruits for salad	⅛ tsp. ground cloves
1 (13 oz.) can pineapple chunks	⅓ cup brown sugar, packed
1 tart apple, unpeeled, cored, and cubed	¼ cup butter or margarine
Juice of 1 lemon	1 cup fresh seedless grapes
¼ teaspoon ground nutmeg	2 bananas, peeled and sliced
¼ tsp. ground cinnamon	

Drain syrup from canned fruit, saving ½ cup. Place canned fruit and apple in a 2½-quart casserole. Add lemon juice, seasonings, and sugar to reserved fruit syrup. Pour over fruit. Dot with butter. Cover and cook 5 minutes. Add grapes and bananas; cover and continue cooking 2 minutes. Serve hot.

Serves 12.

Raspberry Apple Salad
2½ to 3 minutes

1 cup water	1 cup miniature marshmallows
1 (3 oz.) package raspberry gelatin	⅓ cup chopped walnuts
2 cups applesauce	Mayonnaise
Lettuce	Apple wedges
1 cup drained pineapple chunks	Walnut halves

Heat water, 2½ to 3 minutes. Dissolve gelatin in boiling water. Chill until slightly thickened. Add applesauce and pour into 4 individual ring molds. Chill until firm and unmold

on lettuce. Combine pineapple, marshmallows, walnuts, and enough mayonnaise to moisten. Fill centers of molds with pineapple mixture. Garnish with apple wedges and walnut halves. Top with additional mayonnaise.

Serves 4.

Tangy Strawberry Gelatin
6 to 7 minutes

1 (48 oz.) can V-8 juice	½ (5 oz.) bottle horseradish
3 (3 oz.) packages strawberry gelatin	1 ripe avocado, chopped

Pour 3 cups V-8 into small mixing bowl. Heat 6 to 7 minutes. Dissolve gelatin in hot V-8 juice. Add remaining juice. Pour into 7 x 11-inch utility dish, chill until slightly set. Add horseradish and avocado. Refrigerate until ready to serve. Delicious served as an accompaniment to any meat.

Serves 8 to 10.

Cooked Dressing
10 to 11½ minutes

½ cup vinegar	4 egg yolks, beaten
¼ cup sugar	2 tsp. salt
1½ cups milk	1 Tbs. butter or margarine
¼ cup flour	
2 tsp. dry mustard	

Combine vinegar, sugar, and 1 cup milk in 2-quart casserole dish. Cook to a boil, 5 to 6 minutes. Mix flour and mustard with the remaining ½ cup milk. Stir well; add to hot vinegar mixture. Cook 3½ minutes, stirring every 30 seconds. Stir half the hot mixture into egg yolks, then stir all together. Cook to a boil, 1½ to 2 minutes. Remove from oven, add salt and butter, and stir well. Dilute with equal amounts of sour cream, whipped cream, or mayonnaise when using for potato, cabbage, or other hearty salads.

Makes 2 cups.

Cherry Dressing for Coleslaw

2 to 3 minutes

1 (8 oz.) jar red maraschino cherries	½ cup honey
	3 Tbs. light cream
1 egg, well beaten	Dash of salt
¼ cup orange juice	Shredded cabbage

Drain cherries well on paper towel. Combine egg, orange juice, and honey in 1-quart bowl or measurer; stir (use wooden spoon that can be left in oven). Cook until thickened, 2 to 3 minutes, stirring after each minute. Cool. Add cream, salt, and cherries; blend well. Chill thoroughly. Toss with shredded cabbage.

Use red cherries for Washington's Birthday; green for St. Patrick's Day.

Makes 1 cup.

Cherry Dressing for Coleslaw

Roast in Rock Salt

5
Meats

The most important thing to remember when cooking meats by microwave is that they continue to cook after being removed from the oven. Allow large pieces of meat to stand 10 to 20 minutes after cooking. Cover with foil to retain heat. Use a meat thermometer to check the temperature of meat during this standing time. *Do not* put thermometer into oven when oven is turned on.

For best results, select a tender cut of meat that is uniform in size. If it is not, cover the small end with a smooth piece of foil for the first half of the cooking time. Foil can be used for small end of ham or ends of meat loaf also.

Roasts should be turned after half the cooking time. Start with the fat side down except for standing beef rib, which is treated differently in different ovens. Cover meat with wax paper or paper toweling during last half of cooking time to avoid spattering.

The top of the 1½-quart dish of the 4-piece refrigerator and freezer set made by Pyrex is the best trivet for meats in the microwave. A small plate or saucer turned upside down or an oblong or round casserole dish lid can also be used.

To brown meats when the oven has no browning unit, try Kitchen Bouquet diluted with water or salad oil. Also try Adolph's Brown 'n Season, paprika, or seasoned pepper. Or place meat under a preheated conventional broiler after cooking.

Meat Roasting Chart*

	Kind of Meat	Minutes per Pound	Internal Temperature after Standing Time
Beef	Rolled or standing rib	Rare—5 to 6 min.	140°
		Medium—6 to 7 min.	160°
		Well-done—7 to 8 min.	170°
Pork	All roasts	Well-done—9 to 10 min.	185°
Ham	Precooked half	Well-done—5 to 6 min.	130°
	Precooked whole	Well-done—8 to 9 min.	130°
Lamb	Rolled	Well-done—8 to 9 min.	180°
	Leg with bone	Well-done—7 to 8 min.	180°
Veal	All roasts	Well-done—8 to 9 min.	180°

*Based on refrigerated meats of average shape and cut. Times given allow for 20 minutes standing time during which meat will increase in temperature about 20°.

Roast in Rock Salt

1 (4 to 5 lb.) rolled beef roast	1 large (14 x 20 in.) Brown-in-Bag
6 garlic buds, cut in strips	1 (5 lb.) bag rock salt
Pepper	
2 onions, cut in thick slices	

Putting it together

With point of sharp knife, punch slits in roast; push strips of garlic into slits. Place pieces of garlic on all sides of roast. Pepper roast, using twice as much as you usually use (it comes off with salt). Pour 1½ to 2 inches of salt in bottom of roast-in bag that is placed in 3-quart casserole or large utility dish. Spread bag out so salt covers area as large as fat side of roast. Place half of the onion slices on top of salt; place roast on top of onion slices; put remaining onion slices on top of roast. Spread top of bag open and pour salt over roast. Pat in place so that roast is completely covered with about 2 inches of salt on all sides. Close top of bag with string or rubber band, pulling bag tight so salt stays in place. Make 2 holes in bag on top side. Salt will harden when hot and stay on roast when roast is turned. Cook according to chart in your cookbook (roast is best rare or medium).

When roast is finished cooking, let stand 10 minutes. Remove roast from dish close to sink so that salt can be scraped off easily, being careful because salt will be very hot. Salt comes off in large pieces, so use a vegetable brush to clean roast well. Carve and serve the best roast you will ever taste.

Removing the salt

Leftover Beef Stew
30 to 45 minutes

3 cups cooked beef, cubed	1 (2 lb.) package frozen stew vegetables
2 cups gravy, leftover, canned, or packaged gravy mix	Salt and pepper to taste

Put cooked beef in center of 3-quart casserole dish. Pour gravy over meat. Add frozen vegetables around meat, pushing down into gravy. Cover and cook 30 to 45 minutes, stirring after each 10 minutes. Let stand 5 to 10 minutes, covered, before serving.

Serves 8.

Teriyaki Steaks on Skewers
5 minutes

1½ lbs. sirloin steak, ½ in. thick	½ cup soy sauce
1 clove garlic, mashed	1 tsp. sugar
1 Tbs. fresh ginger, chopped	1 small onion, chopped
	8 whole fresh mushrooms

Cut steak diagonally into ¼-inch strips and lace onto wooden skewers. Combine garlic, ginger, soy sauce, sugar, and onion. Marinate skewered steak for 20 minutes. Add whole mushroom to each end of skewer and place skewers across a 7 x 11-inch utility dish. Cook 3 minutes; turn and cook 2 minutes on second side.

Cherry tomatoes, pieces of green pepper, or small pearl onions may also be used on skewers. Increase time slightly if you add any other ingredients. Steak can also be left whole, marinated, and cooked in an oblong dish. Allow a little more time to cook to desired doneness.

Serves 4.

Hamburger Stroganoff
12 to 16 minutes

1 lb. ground beef, chuck or round	1 can undiluted cream of mushroom or cream of chicken soup
½ cup minced onion	
1 clove garlic, minced	2 Tbs. sherry wine
2 Tbs. flour	1 cup cottage cheese, blended until smooth
1½ tsp. salt	
¼ tsp. pepper	
¼ tsp. paprika	Snipped fresh parsley, chives, or dill
1 (4 oz.) can sliced mushrooms, drained	

Place first 8 ingredients in a 2-quart casserole dish. Break up meat with a fork. Stir well. Cook 6 to 8 minutes, stirring once. Add soup and sherry. Cook 4 to 6 minutes. Add cottage cheese, stir well, and cook 2 minutes. Sprinkle with parsley. Serve over hot noodles or rice.

Serves 6.

Pizza Hamburger Pie
8 to 8½ minutes

1 lb. lean ground beef	1 (8 oz.) can tomato sauce
1½ tsp. salt	2 Tbs. minced onion
¼ tsp. pepper	1 cup grated mozzarella cheese
1 tsp. horseradish	
1 tsp. Worcestershire sauce	2 Tbs. minced parsley
1 tsp. prepared mustard	½ tsp. basil
	¼ tsp. oregano

Teriyaki Steaks on Skewers

Pizza Hamburger Pie

Combine lamb cubes with all ingredients except green peppers, mix thoroughly, cover, and let stand for 6 to 8 hours or overnight in refrigerator. Place lamb cubes alternately on wooden skewers with green pepper. Lay skewers across 7 x 11-inch baking dish. Cook 8 skewers at a time for 6 to 8 minutes. Repeat with remaining meat and peppers. Meat may be basted with sauce during cooking. Serve with rice.

Serves 6.

Little Mexican Meat Loaves
20 minutes

1 package seasoned coating mix for hamburger	2 Tbs. onion, chopped
2 lbs. ground chuck or round	1 tsp. chili powder
1 (12 oz.) can whole kernel corn with peppers	1 egg, slightly beaten
	½ cup catsup

Lightly toss ground beef with salt, pepper, horseradish, Worcestershire sauce, and mustard. Press meat against sides and bottom of 9-inch glass pie dish. Spread tomato sauce over meat. Sprinkle with onions, cheese, parsley, basil, and oregano. Cook 5 minutes, turn dish, and cook 3 to 3½ minutes. Let stand 5 minutes. Cut into wedges and serve.

If lean ground beef is not used, carefully drain off fat; let stand before serving.

Serves 4.

Lamb Kabobs
6 to 8 minutes

1 leg of lamb (5 to 6 lbs.), deboned and cut in cubes	1 tsp. salt
	¼ tsp. pepper
4 cloves garlic, minced	2 Tbs. vinegar
	3 Tbs. cooking oil
2 tsp. oregano	2 large green peppers, cut in 2-in. cubes
1 pinch cumin	
2 (7 oz.) cans green chili salsa	

Little Mexican Meat Loaves

Empty seasoned coating mix into shaker bag, set aside. Combine beef, corn, onions, chili powder and egg; mix well. Form into 8 round loaves, no more than 2½ inches thick. Carefully shake each loaf separately in shaker bag until evenly coated. Place in 7 x 11-inch utility dish. Bake loaves 10 minutes, turn dish, and cook 10 minutes longer. For ovens with browning unit, brown last 6 to 8 minutes. Remove from oven and top each loaf with 1 tablespoon catsup. Let stand 8 to 10 minutes before serving.

Loaves may be prepared, coated, then refrigerated until ready to bake. Add 1 to 2 minutes to cooking time if chilled. If meat is fatty, drain drippings from dish after ½ of the cooking time.
Serves 8.

Bavarian Meat Balls
15 minutes

1 lb. ground beef round	1 tsp. Worcestershire sauce
½ clove garlic, crushed	Flour
½ medium onion, minced	2 strips bacon, diced
¼ tsp. savory	½ cup strong coffee
½ tsp. salt	½ tsp. sugar
½ cup soft bread crumbs	¼ tsp. salt
1½ tsp. prepared mustard	¼ cup chili sauce
Dash of hot pepper sauce	½ cup water
	2 Tbs. flour
	½ cup sour cream

Combine first 9 ingredients; mix well. Shape into about 15 meatballs; dust with flour. Cook bacon in a 7 x 11-inch utility dish until crisp, 2 minutes. Remove bacon from dish. Cook meat balls in bacon drippings 6 minutes, turning and rotating balls after 3 to 4 minutes.

Remove meat balls from dish. Add coffee, sugar, salt, chili sauce, and water to dish; blend well. Mix flour to a smooth paste with an additional 2 tablespoons water; stir into sauce mixture. Cook and stir until smooth and slightly thickened, 4 minutes, stirring after 2 and 3 minutes. Stir in sour cream, blending well. Add bacon and meat balls, turning balls to coat with sauce. Heat 3 minutes.
Serves 4.

Marinated Pork Tenderloins

4 (8 to 10 oz.) pork loins	½ tsp. garlic powder
1 cup soy sauce	1 Tbs. sesame seeds
6 Tbs. sugar	
1 tsp. pepper	
1 tsp. ground ginger	

Place pork loins in shallow baking dish. Combine all other ingredients in small bowl; stir well. Pour over pork loins, cover. Leave meat in marinade overnight or at least 6 hours, stirring occasionally. Before cooking, pour off marinade. Roll meat in sesame seeds. Cook 8 to 9 minutes per pound. Turn loins after half the cooking time.
Serves 4.

Pork Pieces in Sour Cream
5 to 21 minutes

1 Tbs. butter or margarine	2 Tbs. vinegar
1 lb. pork chunks	1 Tbs. sugar
Seasoned flour or bread crumbs	½ cup dairy sour cream
½ cup water or stock	¼ tsp. savory (optional)
½ bay leaf	

Melt butter in 8-inch square or 1½-quart casserole dish in microwave oven, 30 seconds to 1 minute. Cut meat into 1-inch pieces and coat with flour by shaking it in a paper bag. Roll in butter and cook 5 to 8 minutes, stirring once. Combine remaining ingredients and pour over meat. Cook, covered with plastic wrap, 10 to 13 minutes, stirring once.
Serves 4.

Ham with Honey Sauce

Precooked boneless ham (4 to 5 lbs.)	2 Tbs. brown sugar
Cloves	1 tsp. Liquid Smoke
½ cup honey	
1 Tbs. orange rind	
2 Tbs. vinegar	

Ham with Honey Sauce

Prepare sauce by combining first 5 ingredients in a 1-pint glass jar or 2-cup measurer. Stir and heat, uncovered, 1½ to 2 minutes.

Remove the jelly and cut off most of the fat from the ham. Place ham in a flat dish; spread ⅓ of the sauce over the ham. Cook for ⅓ of the cooking time. Remove ham from oven and score; stud with cloves. Spread more sauce over ham and continue baking, basting several times. Cover any parts of ham that are beginning to overcook with foil, spread smoothly. Cooking time 6 to 7 minutes per pound. Let ham stand 15 minutes before carving. Serve extra sauce with ham, or store in refrigerator, covered for use on ham slices.

Serves 12.

Ham Slices à l'Orange
8 to 12 minutes

6 (2½ to 3 lbs.) slices cooked ham	½ tsp. cinnamon
	½ tsp. nutmeg
1 cup orange juice	½ cup maple syrup
½ cup seedless raisins	

Place ham slices in 7 x 11-inch utility dish. Combine remaining ingredients and pour over ham. Cook, covered with paper towel, 8 to 12 minutes.

Serves 6.

Savory Sausage Ring
15 to 17 minutes

1 egg	¾ tsp. salt
⅔ cup milk	¾ tsp. basil, crushed
¾ cup uncooked quick or old-fashioned oats	½ tsp. sage
	6 canned peach halves, drained
1½ lbs. pork sausage	Scrambled eggs
	Parsley
⅔ cup peeled chopped apple	Crab apples (canned)

Combine egg, milk, and oats. Let stand 5 minutes. Add sausage, apple, and seasonings. Place a custard cup in center of 3-quart casserole dish. Arrange peach halves, cut side up, in bottom of casserole around custard cup. Spoon the sausage mixture over the peaches and pack uniformly, leaving cup empty. Cover with paper towels. Bake 15 to 17 minutes, turning dish once after 7 minutes. Drain off fat. Let stand 5 to 10 minutes. Turn into serving platter. Spoon scrambled eggs into center of ring. Garnish with parsley and crab apples.

Serves 6.

6
Fish and Seafood

Fish cooked in a microwave oven is delicate in flavor and texture. Be careful to cook the fish only until it can be flaked with a fork; overcooking toughens fish.

You can defrost frozen fish fillets by placing the frozen package (unless wrapped in foil) in the microwave oven on a paper towel. Defrost a 1-pound package for 2 to 4 minutes, turning the package at least once during thawing. Remove from oven and let stand 10 to 15 minutes longer, or separate fillets under cold running water. Too much thawing may cook the fish.

Baked Albacore
10 to 12 minutes

1½ to 2 lbs. albacore fillets	¼ tsp. rosemary
¾ cup salad oil	¼ tsp. thyme
⅓ cup lemon juice	¼ tsp. oregano
2 Tbs. wine vinegar	¼ tsp. sweet basil
1 Tbs. Accent	⅓ to ½ tsp. salt
1 tsp. garlic powder	

Cut albacore fillet in half crosswise. Place in shallow 7 x 11-inch utility dish. Combine remaining ingredients and pour over fish. Cover tightly with plastic wrap. (If possible, marinate in refrigerator 4 to 5 hours or overnight before cooking.) Bake 5 to 6 minutes. Turn and baste; cook 5 to 6 minutes longer.

Let stand covered 15 to 20 more minutes before serving. Serve with a hot salad oil-lemon juice sauce.

Serves 6.

Deviled Crab

7¹⁄₆ to 8¾ minutes

1½ cups fresh or
   canned
   crabmeat
1 Tbs. butter or
   margarine
¼ cup cracker
   crumbs
¾ cup milk
2 eggs, beaten

¼ tsp. salt
¾ tsp. dry
   mustard
1 tsp.
   horseradish
Dash of cayenne
   pepper
Dash of hot pepper
   sauce
Paprika

Flake crabmeat, remove fibers, and set aside. Melt butter in an 8-inch glass cake dish for 10 to 15 seconds. Add cracker crumbs and milk. Cook 4 minutes, stirring after 2 minutes. Add beaten eggs and remaining ingredients except paprika. Cook 1 to 1½ minutes. Add crabmeat. Sprinkle with paprika and heat thoroughly, 2 to 3 minutes. Or transfer to individual crab shells or ramekins before heating.

Serves 4.

Baked Fish Turbans

9 to 10 minutes

4 (1 lb.) halibut or
   other white fish
   fillets
Salt and pepper
½ cup chopped
   celery
¼ cup chopped
   green pepper

½ cup clam or
   tomato and clam
   juice
¼ cup prepared
   mustard
Paprika or parsley
   flakes

Baked Fish Turbans

Sprinkle fillets with salt and pepper. Mix celery and green pepper and spoon onto fish; roll fillets. Place in 8-inch square glass baking dish. Bake 6 minutes, turning dish once. Combine clam juice and mustard. Pour over fish turbans. Bake 3 to 4 minutes longer. Sprinkle with paprika or parsley flakes and serve.

Serves 4.

Tomato-Fish Bake with Beans and Rice

15 to 16½ minutes

1 lb. fish fillets
1 cup chopped
   onion
2 Tbs. margarine
   or cooking oil
1 Tbs. flour
½ tsp. salt
Dash of pepper
1 can (1 lb.)
   tomatoes

2 Tbs. brown
   sugar
2 Tbs. vinegar
1 tsp. prepared
   mustard
1 can (1 lb.)
   kidney beans,
   drained
1½ cups hot cooked
   rice

Cut fish into 1-inch pieces, set aside. In a 7 x 11-inch baking dish, cook onions in margarine or oil 3 minutes. Stir in flour, salt, and pepper. Add tomatoes, brown sugar, vinegar, and mustard. Mix well and cook 5 minutes, stirring twice. Add fish, cover with plastic wrap, and cook 5 to 6 minutes, or until fish flakes easily.

In a separate dish, stir kidney beans into hot rice. Cook 2 to 2½ minutes. Serve fish over beans and rice.

Serves 4.

Salmon Steaks

5 to 10 minutes

6 (2 lbs.) salmon
   steaks
¼ cup butter or
   margarine
1 tsp. salt

1 tsp. seasoned
   pepper
6 lemon slices
6 onion slices
Paprika

Place steaks in 7 x 11-inch utility dish. Spread each piece with butter; sprinkle with salt and seasoned pepper. Put a lemon slice and an onion slice on each piece of fish. Sprinkle with paprika. Cook 5 to 10 minutes, until fish flakes easily with a fork.

Serves 6.

Scallop Rarebit
10 minutes

1 lb. scallops, fresh or frozen
2 Tbs. butter or margarine
2 Tbs. flour
1 tsp. salt
Dash of pepper
⅔ cup water
⅓ cup catsup
1 Tbs. mustard
2 cups grated cheddar cheese
2 eggs, beaten
2 Tbs. chopped parsley
Toast points

Thaw frozen scallops. Remove any shell particles and wash. Cut scallops into ½-inch pieces. Place in a 1½-quart casserole dish; add butter. Cook 2½ minutes. Blend in flour, salt, and pepper. Add water gradually and cook 3 minutes, until thick, stirring once. Add catsup, mustard, and cheese; heat 2 minutes.

Stir a little of the hot sauce into beaten eggs; add to remaining sauce with scallops. Heat 2½ minutes. Add parsley. Serve on toast points.
Serves 6.

Saucy Shrimp Squares
12½ to 15¾ minutes

1 tsp. butter or margarine
3 eggs, beaten
1½ cups milk
4 slices bread, cut in cubes
1 (4½ oz.) can shrimp, drained
2 Tbs. parsley
1 Tbs. lemon juice
¼ tsp. salt
Dash of pepper

Melt butter in 8-inch square glass dish for 30 to 45 seconds. Combine beaten eggs and milk. Add bread cubes, shrimp, parsley, lemon juice, salt, and pepper. Cook 12 to 15 minutes, until set. Serve with cheese sauce.
Serves 4.

Cheese Sauce
4 to 4¾ minutes

1 Tbs. butter
1 Tbs. flour
¼ tsp. salt
1 cup milk
1 cup grated cheese

Saucy Shrimp Squares

Melt butter in 1-quart casserole dish for 30 to 45 seconds. Stir in flour and salt and blend to a smooth paste. Add milk gradually, stirring all the time. Cook until hot, 2½ to 3 minutes. Stir after first minute and then every 30 seconds. Add cheese and cook 1 minute, until cheese melts and sauce is hot. Stir well before serving.

Luncheon Shrimp and Crab Bake
7 to 9 minutes

1 can (10½ oz.) shrimp soup, undiluted
1 (6½ to 7½ oz.) can crab meat, drained and flaked
1 (4½ to 5 oz.) can medium shrimp, drained
1 cup diced celery
½ cup diced onion
½ cup diced green pepper
1½ tsp. Worcestershire sauce
2 Tbs. sherry
½ tsp. salt
Dash of pepper
1 cup crushed potato chips

Combine all ingredients, except potato chips, in 1½-quart casserole with soup. Mix well. Sprinkle potato chips over mixture. Cook until hot, 7 to 9 minutes.
Serves 6.

Luncheon Shrimp and Crab Bake

Baked Stuffed Trout

Sole Parmesan
6 to 8 minutes

1½ lbs. fillet of sole or halibut	¼ cup Parmesan cheese
1 (10 oz.) can cream of shrimp soup, undiluted	Paprika Butter or margarine Parsley
Dash of cayenne	Lemon wedges

Place the fillets in buttered 7 x 11-inch utility dish. Pour soup over fish. Sprinkle with cayenne, cheese, and paprika. Dot with butter. Bake 6 to 8 minutes. Garnish with parsley and lemon wedges.

Serves 4.

Baked Stuffed Trout
10½ to 12¾ minutes

2½ lbs. (4 to 5) trout	Paprika Onion powder
¼ cup melted butter	2 cups prepared stuffing mix, mixed as directed
Salt	
Pepper	

Wash fish, wipe dry. Melt butter in oven 30 to 45 seconds; brush inside of fish with ½ of the butter, lightly sprinkle inside with salt. Fill cavity with stuffing. Close, using wooden toothpicks. Brush outside of fish with remaining butter. Sprinkle with pepper, paprika, and onion powder. Arrange in 7 x 11-inch glass baking dish. Cook 10 to 12 minutes. Turn dish after half the cooking time.

Serves 4 to 5.

Tuna Tater Tempters
8 to 9½ minutes

1 cup instant mashed potato flakes	¼ tsp. salt ¼ tsp. garlic salt
1 can (9¼ oz.) drained tuna	1 cup cornflakes, finely crushed, or ⅓ cup cornflake crumbs
1 egg	
½ cup milk	
⅓ cup finely chopped celery	½ tsp. seasoned salt
2 Tbs. chopped pimiento	1 can (10½ oz.) condensed cream of mushroom soup
1 Tbs. instant minced onion or ¼ cup chopped fresh onion	⅓ cup milk

In medium mixing bowl combine potato flakes, tuna, egg, milk, celery, pimiento, minced onion, salt, and garlic salt. Stir by hand until combined. Form into about 12 balls, 2 inches in diameter. Combine crushed cornflakes and seasoned salt. Coat tuna balls with seasoned cornflakes. Place in 8-inch baking dish and cook 6 to 7 minutes, turning balls every 2 minutes.

Prepare sauce by combining soup and milk in 1-quart bowl or measuring cup. Heat 2 to 2½ minutes. Stir well. Pour over tuna and serve hot.

Serves 6.

7
Poultry and Eggs

Poultry

The cooking time for poultry will vary according to its size and age. Stewing chickens should not be cooked in a microwave oven. Arrange chicken pieces in the dish so that larger pieces are toward the outside. Rotate the pieces for even cooking.

Before cooking, brush poultry with melted butter, shortening, or a sauce. Cover small ends with foil to prevent overcooking. If your oven has no browning unit, try using a browning agent such as Gold 'n Crust or Kitchen Bouquet, diluted with salad oil, or soy sauce.

Arroz con Pollo
29 to 32 minutes

2½ to 3 lbs. frying chicken pieces	1 tsp. salt
1 Tbs. olive oil	4 canned tomatoes, drained and
1 onion, chopped	chopped
1 clove garlic, minced	1½ cups water
1 bay leaf	1 (2 oz.) can tiny green peas
Generous pinch of saffron	1 jar (2 oz.) pimientos
1½ cups quick-cooking rice	6 green pepper strips

Place chicken pieces in a 4-quart casserole dish. Add oil, onion, garlic, bay leaf, saffron, rice, salt, tomatoes, and water. Stir to coat rice with liquid. Cover and cook 28 to 30 minutes. Arrange chicken pieces around edge of large platter. Heap rice in center.

Heat peas in a small covered dish, 1 to 2 minutes. Drain peas and pour over rice (make a pocket in center of rice). Garnish with pimiento and green pepper.

Serves 6.

Arroz con Pollo

Chicken à l'Orange
22½ to 24½ minutes

4 frying chicken legs	½ cup onion, minced
4 frying chicken thighs	⅔ cup chicken broth
⅓ cup flour	1 cup fresh orange juice
1 tsp. salt	1 tsp. grated orange peel
¼ tsp. pepper	Fresh orange slices
¼ cup butter or margarine	

Shake chicken pieces in plastic bag with flour, salt, and pepper. Set aside. In 7 x 11-inch baking dish melt butter, 30 seconds. Add onion and cook 2 minutes. Sprinkle in flour mixture remaining from coating chicken. Stir and blend well. Gradually stir in chicken broth, orange juice and peel. Cook 2 minutes, stirring every 30 seconds. Arrange chicken pieces in sauce, spoon sauce over chicken, cover with wax paper, and cook 18 to 20 minutes.

Garnish chicken with orange slices. Serve with orange gravy over rice.

Serves 4.

Chicken Cacciatore

Chicken Cacciatore
30 to 35 minutes

2½ lbs. frying chicken pieces	¼ lb. mushrooms, sliced
1 (16 oz.) can solid pack tomatoes	½ cup water or ¼ cup water and ¼ cup wine
1 (6 oz.) can tomato paste	¼ tsp. thyme
½ cup chopped onion	½ tsp. oregano leaves, crushed
¾ cup chopped green pepper	1 bay leaf
1 clove garlic, minced	1 tsp. salt
	¼ tsp. pepper

Wash and dry chicken and set aside. Combine all remaining ingredients in a 2½-quart casserole. Stir to break tomatoes. Add chicken pieces, stirring until chicken is coated. Cover and cook 30 to 35 minutes, stirring once. Remove bay leaf. Serve with rice, noodles, or spaghetti.

Serves 4 to 6.

Chicken Divan
22 minutes

1 lb. fresh broccoli
or 1 (10 oz.)
package frozen
broccoli spears
2 chicken breasts,
halved
1 (10 oz.) can
cream of chicken
soup

½ cup mayonnaise
1 tsp. lemon juice
½ tsp. curry
powder
½ cup grated sharp
cheese
Paprika

Wash and split large pieces of broccoli. Cut several times into stem end to hasten cooking. Arrange fresh or frozen spears in 7 x 11-inch utility dish. Cover and cook 8 minutes. Place chicken breast halves in another 7 x 11-inch utility dish. Cover with paper towel and cook 5 minutes, then turn chicken and cook 5 minutes longer.

Skin, bone, and slice cooked chicken breasts. Arrange on top of broccoli spears. Combine soup, mayonnaise, lemon juice, and curry powder. Pour over chicken. Sprinkle with cheese and paprika. Bake 4 minutes, turning dish once.

Serves 4.

Chicken Teriyaki
14 to 16 minutes

1½ lbs. chicken
pieces
⅔ cup soy sauce
½ cup white wine
2 Tbs. sugar

½ tsp. ground
ginger
1 clove garlic,
chopped

Place chicken in 7 x 11-inch utility dish skin side down, with larger pieces toward outside of dish. Mix all other ingredients in small bowl, stirring to dissolve sugar; pour over chicken. Marinate for 2 hours, turning and basting occasionally. Cook, basting occasionally, 7 to 8 minutes. Move larger pieces to center of dish and cook 7 to 8 minutes longer.

Serves 6.

Quick Chicken Italian
28 to 30 minutes

2½ to 3 lbs. frying
chicken, cut up
1 (1½ oz.)
envelope
spaghetti sauce
mix
1 (8 oz.) can
tomato sauce

1 cup water or ¾
cup water and
¼ cup wine
1 Tbs. oregano
(optional)
2 Tbs. parsley
(optional)

Chicken Teriyaki

Quick Chicken Italian

Cut chicken into uniform pieces and set aside. Combine sauce mix, tomato sauce, and water. Stir in chicken pieces, coating with sauce. Cover and cook 28 to 30 minutes.

Serves 4.

Chicken Livers
12½ to 17 minutes

⅓ cup all-purpose flour	4 large mushrooms, sliced
1 tsp. salt	
¼ tsp. pepper	½ cup green onion, chopped
¼ tsp. monosodium glutamate (optional)	2 stalks celery, cut on the diagonal
1 lb. chicken livers, cut in fourths	1 cup milk
	¼ cup sherry
½ cup butter or margarine	

Combine flour, salt, pepper and MSG. Dredge chicken livers in seasoned flour. In 8-inch round cake dish, melt butter, 30 seconds to 1 minute. Add livers, stir, and cook 3 to 4 minutes. Stir, then cook 3 to 4 minutes longer. Add mushrooms, green onions, and celery. Cook 3 to 4 minutes. Add milk and sherry, blending well. Cook until thickened and heated through, 3 to 4 minutes, stirring once.

Serve on hot rice or Chinese noodles.

Serves 6.

Stuffed Roast Duckling
44 minutes

3 cups dried bread cubes, toasted	1 egg, beaten
	½ tsp. salt
½ cup boiling water	Dash of pepper
2 tsp. grated orange rind	½ tsp. poultry seasoning
⅔ cups diced orange	5-lb. duckling, at room temperature
2 cups diced celery	Salt
¼ cup melted butter or margarine	

Soften bread cubes in hot water for 15 seconds. Add remaining ingredients; combine lightly.

Wash duckling and pat dry. Rub cavity with salt. Stuff loosely with stuffing. Close opening with toothpicks or wooden skewers. Tie legs together to tail. Tie wings close to the body. Lightly salt outside of duck. Cover wings and small end of legs and tail with aluminum foil.

Place duckling in 2-quart utility dish, breast side up. Cook 22 minutes, turning once. Remove foil from wings and legs. Baste duckling with drippings in dish. Turn breast side down. Pour off excess fat when duckling is turned. Cook 22 minutes, turning dish once. Baste once or twice during the cooking on the second side.

Remove from oven and allow to stand 20 minutes before carving.

Barbecued Cornish Hens
24 minutes

2 Cornish hens, split in half
½ cup barbecue sauce

Place Cornish hens skin side down in a 7 x 11-inch utility dish. Brush half the barbecue sauce on the hens. Cook 12 minutes. Turn skin side up, brush with remaining sauce. Cook 12 minutes.

Serves 4.

Roast Turkey

1 8 to 15-lb. turkey with giblets removed	Stuffing recipe
	Melted butter or vegetable oil
Salt	

Wash turkey. Sprinkle inside with salt. Stuff if desired. Close opening with toothpicks. Tie legs together and wings to sides with string. Brushed with butter or oil. Cover legs and wings with small pieces of foil. Place turkey breast side down in baking dish. Cook uncovered for half of cooking time. Turn bird (use paper towels), remove foil, and continue cooking remaining time. Wax paper or paper towel-

Most ovens are built to accommodate a full-size turkey.

ing can be used in oven to prevent spattering.

Remove from oven and allow 15 minutes standing time. Before carving, test for doneness. Internal temperature should be 175° when turkey is removed from oven, 190° after standing time.

Cooking Times (Stuffed or Unstuffed)

8 to 10 lbs.	7½ min. per lb.
10 to 12 lbs.	7 min. per lb.
12 to 15 lbs.	6½ min. per lb.

Turkey Stuffing
4 to 5 minutes

1½ cups chopped celery	1½ Tbs. salt
¾ cup chopped onion	½ tsp. pepper
1 cup melted butter or margarine	½ tsp. poultry seasoning
10 cups bread cubes	1 cup warm water

Cook celery and onion in butter until soft, 4 to 5 minutes. Put bread cubes in bowl and add seasonings. Pour in cooked vegetables, add water, and mix. Stuff turkey lightly, both body and neck cavity. Sew up openings with heavy thread or lace closed, using toothpicks for skewers.

For a 12 to 14-pound turkey.

Chestnut Stuffing
21 to 28 minutes

1½ to 2 lbs. fresh chestnuts	3 cups bread crumbs or corn bread
4 Tbs. butter or margarine	¼ cup chopped parsley
1 cup chopped onion	1 tsp. salt
1 cup chopped celery	¼ tsp. pepper
1 lb. sausage meat	Warm water

Wash chestnuts and make two slits in outer shell. Place in 3-quart baking dish, cover with cold water, and place in oven. Boil 4 to 5 minutes. Remove nuts one by one and remove shells and inner skins with sharp knife. Cover peeled nuts with hot water and cook covered 8 to 12 minutes longer. Drain and cut into pieces. Should make 2 cups.

Cook butter, onion, and celery in an 8-inch round baking dish until soft, 4 to 5 minutes. Add sausage, crumbled. Cook covered with a paper towel 5 to 6 minutes, stirring several times. Drain off fat. Add chestnuts and other ingredients and combine in a large mixing bowl. Mix well. If stuffing appears too dry, add a little warm water. Stuff loosely into neck and body cavities of turkey. Sew up openings or lace closed; don't use metal skewers.

For a 10 to 12-pound turkey.

Turkey Tetrazzini
14 minutes

7 oz. thin spaghetti	2 cans cream of chicken soup
2 cans (8 oz.) mushroom pieces, drained	2 cups sour cream
½ cup butter or margarine	Parmesan cheese
2 cups cooked turkey or chicken, diced	

Break spaghetti into 1-inch pieces. Cook and drain. In 2½-quart casserole, combine spaghetti, mushrooms, butter, turkey, soup, and sour cream. Cook uncovered 6 minutes. Stir, cook 6 more minutes. Add cheese and cook 2 minutes longer.

Serves 8 to 12.

Turkey Tetrazzini

Eggs

Eggs cook in a very short time in the microwave oven. They also continue to cook when removed from the oven, so care must be taken not to overcook. Excessive steam might build up and cause the egg to pop and splatter out of its dish.

Cooking times will vary with the size, temperature, and number of eggs prepared at one time. Remove eggs from the oven while still slightly underdone and allow them to stand covered to complete cooking.

Scrambled Eggs
3 to 3½ minutes

6 eggs	Dash of pepper
⅓ cup milk	2 Tbs. butter or margarine
¼ tsp. salt	

Beat eggs. Add milk, salt, and pepper. Melt butter in 10-inch round pie dish. Pour egg mixture into dish. Cook 1 minute. Stir, cook 2 to 2½ minutes longer, stirring every 30 seconds.

Cheese Scrambled Eggs

Add 1 tablespoon grated cheddar cheese for each egg.

Bacon Scrambled Eggs

Add crumbled bacon or imitation bacon bits to eggs after cooking, 1 tablespoon for each egg.

Ham and Scrambled Eggs

Add chopped cooked ham or canned Spam, heated in microwave oven, to cooked, scrambled eggs, 1 tablespoon for each egg.

Mushroom Scrambled Eggs

Saute sliced mushroom, canned or fresh, in microwave oven. Add 1 tablespoon for each egg.

Herbed Scrambled Eggs

Add 1 tablespoon chopped parsley, 1 tablespoon chopped chives, and a dash of thyme, crushed, to egg mixture before cooking.

Scrambled Eggs with Bacon, Green Pepper, and Onion

Cook 5 slices of bacon in microwave oven. Crumble and set aside. Drain all but 2 tablespoons of fat. Add 2 tablespoons diced green pepper and 2½ tablespoons chopped onion to drippings. Sauté in microwave oven for 1 to 2 minutes before adding egg mixture. Garnish with crumbled bacon.

Dried Beef and Scrambled Eggs

Frizzle cut-up dried beef, 2 tablespoons per egg, in butter before adding egg mixture.

Serves 4.

Green Chilis and Eggs
7½ to 9 minutes

¼ lb. mushrooms, sliced	¼ tsp. salt
4 Tbs. butter or margarine	⅛ tsp. pepper
8 eggs	½ cup shredded Jack cheese
2 Tbs. canned diced green chilis	Tomato slices
6 Tbs. milk	⅓ cup thinly sliced green onion

In a small bowl cook mushrooms in 2 tablespoons of the butter or margarine, covered, 2 to 3 minutes, stirring twice. Set aside. Melt remaining 2 tablespoons butter in a 10-inch glass skillet or 1½-quart casserole, 25 to 30 seconds. Add eggs, chilis, milk, salt, and pepper; mix with fork to scramble. Cover and cook 5 to 5½ minutes, stirring after every 2 minutes. Stir eggs when done to your liking. Transfer to a serving platter, top with mushrooms, ½ of the cheese, tomato slices, then remaining cheese and onion.

Serves 4.

Green Chilis and Eggs

Creamed Eggs and Mushrooms
4 to 5 minutes

1 Tbs. butter or margarine	1 4-oz. can sliced mushrooms
1 Tbs. flour	Evaporated milk
½ tsp. salt	4 hard-cooked eggs, chopped
Dash of pepper	
1 Tbs. minced onion	

Melt butter in microwave oven in a 1½-quart casserole, 30 seconds. Stir in flour, salt, pepper, and onion. Drain mushroom liquid into a measuring cup; add enough milk to make one cup. Reserve mushrooms. Add liquid to white sauce base, stirring well. Cook 1 minute, stir, and cook 1½ to 2 minutes longer, stirring every 30 seconds. Stir in mushrooms and eggs. Heat 1 to 1½ minutes, stirring every 30 seconds.

You can substitute 6 ounces of fresh mushrooms, washed and sliced and sautéed in the butter before adding the flour. Use 1 cup of milk or diluted evaporated milk.

Serves 6.

Eggs and Asparagus in Cheese Sauce
14½ to 17½ minutes

2 (10 oz.) packages frozen cut asparagus	1¾ cups milk
3 Tbs. butter or margarine	1 cup shredded sharp cheddar cheese
3 Tbs. flour	6 hard-cooked eggs, sliced
½ tsp. salt	Hot toast points
Dash of pepper	

Cook asparagus in a 1½-quart covered casserole, 10 to 11 minutes. Melt butter in a 2-quart baking dish, 30 seconds. Blend in flour, salt, and pepper. Add milk gradually, stirring constantly. Cook 2 to 3 minutes, stirring every 30 seconds. Stir in ¾ cup cheese and asparagus. Add eggs, reserving a few slices for garnish. Heat 2 to 3 minutes. Sprinkle with remaining cheese and garnish with egg slices. Serve with toast.

Serves 4.

8
One-Dish Meals

Many casseroles call for starchy foods such as noodles or rice. These can be cooked in the microwave oven, but they take about the same time as with conventional cooking. So you can save time by cooking them on top of your range while preparing another part of the recipe in your microwave.

Always use the size dish recommended in the recipe, and increase the size as you increase the recipe. A double recipe usually takes 1½ times as long to cook, but it is wise to check before the time is up, to avoid overcooking. Be especially careful not to overcook dishes containing cheese or eggs, or you will have rubbery, tough cheese and dry, hard eggs.

Most casseroles, especially larger ones, should be stirred lightly from time to time to insure even cooking. If stirring isn't advisable, turn the dish several times, or, if the outside edges seem to be cooking too quickly, cover them with foil until the center is done.

If the recipe calls for a topping, add it after stirring, or, if it just needs to melt, add it after cooking. Crushed potato chips are an excellent topping, and make the casserole look browner on top.

You can prepare casseroles ahead of time and reheat just before serving; be sure to stir during reheating time. Frozen casseroles can be thawed and heated in the microwave. Allow about half again as much time as for normal cooking, stir or turn as required, and watch out for overcooking.

Three Bean and Frank Barbecue
12 to 13 minutes

1 (10 oz.) package frozen lima beans
¼ cup water
1 (1 lb.) can pork and beans
1 (1 lb.) can red kidney beans, drained
½ cup catsup
¼ cup molasses
1 tsp. dry mustard
½ tsp. Worcestershire sauce
½ (1⅝ oz.) envelope onion soup mix
1 lb. frankfurters, cut in 1-in. pieces

Add water to lima beans in 1½-quart covered casserole. Cook 7 minutes. Drain and mix in remaining ingredients. Cover and cook 5 to 6 minutes, or until bubbly and hot.
Serves 6.

Three Bean and Frank Barbecue

Stuffed Cabbage Rolls

Stuffed Cabbage Rolls
22 to 27 minutes

12 large cabbage leaves	¼ cup milk
1 lb. lean ground beef	1 tsp. seasoned salt
¼ lb. lean ground pork	¼ tsp. pepper
¼ cup finely chopped onion	⅛ tsp. allspice
1 cup cooked rice	1 (8 oz.) can tomato paste
2 Tbs. chopped parsley	½ cup dry white wine
1 egg	¼ cup finely chopped onion
	1 whole clove
	1 small bay leaf

Place cabbage leaves in covered casserole and cook 4 to 6 minutes or until slightly limp. In 2-quart casserole, combine beef, pork, and onion. Cook 3 to 4 minutes or until no longer pink. Add rice, parsley, egg, milk, seasoned salt, pepper, and allspice to meat mixture; mix well. Place ¼ cup of meat mixture on each cabbage leaf. Fold sides of leaf over stuffing and roll up. Set aside. In 1-quart bowl, combine tomato paste, wine, onion, clove, and bay leaf. Cook, covered, 3 minutes. Arrange cabbage rolls in 7 x 11-inch baking dish, seam side down. Pour sauce over rolls, cover with wax paper, and cook 12 to 14 minutes or until cabbage is tender.

Serves 4 to 6.

Quick Chili
12 to 15 minutes

1 lb. ground round or chuck beef	¼ tsp. garlic powder
½ tsp. salt	1 Tbs. chili powder
1 tsp. onion powder	1 (2 lb. 8 oz.) can chili with beans

Place meat in 3-quart casserole dish. Cook until just slightly pink, 5 to 6 minutes, stirring several times. Add salt, onion, garlic, and chili powders and canned chili. Cook until hot, 7 to 9 minutes, stirring once.

Or use 1 pound of meat 3 (1 pound) cans of chili beans, with an additional tablespoon of chili powder. Cooking time will be the same.

Serves 6.

Eggplant Moussaka
21 to 24 minutes

1 medium eggplant, cut into 8 slices	¼ tsp. pepper
	½ cup Parmesan cheese
Salad oil	Béchamel sauce
1 lb. ground beef	
1 tsp. salt	

Slice eggplant without peeling, about ½ inch thick. Brush each slice with oil and place in 7 x 11-inch utility dish, placing extra pieces on top. Cook 5 minutes, turn, cook 4 minutes longer. Break ground beef into small chunks in 1½-

quart casserole dish; add salt and pepper. Cook until meat loses redness, 3 minutes, stir, cook 1 to 2 minutes longer. Place 4 eggplant slices in bottom of 8-inch square baking dish. Put meat on top; place remaining eggplant over meat. Pour sauce over and sprinkle with Parmesan cheese. Heat 8 to 10 minutes, turning dish after 4 minutes. Browning unit may be used for the last 4 minutes.

Serves 4.

Chicken Enchilada Casserole
16½ to 19 minutes

1 (6 oz.) can pitted ripe olives	½ cup olive liquid
	2 tsp. chili powder
2 cups chopped onion	1 tsp. salt
1 large garlic clove, minced	½ tsp. sugar
	2½ cups cubed cooked chicken
1 Tbs. cooking oil	
1 (1 lb.) can tomatoes, drained and chopped	2 Tbs. chopped parsley
	6 corn tortillas
	1½ cups grated cheddar cheese
1 (6 oz.) can tomato paste	

Drain olives, reserving liquid, and cut in quarters. Cook onion and garlic in oil in 1½-quart casserole for 3 minutes. Add tomatoes, tomato paste, ½ cup olive liquid, chili powder, salt, and sugar. Cover and cook 3 minutes. Stir in chicken, parsley, and olives and set aside. Spread tortillas on paper toweling in oven; heat 30 seconds to 1 minute. In a 2-quart casserole, layer sauce with chicken, tortillas, and cheese, ending with a tortilla cut in quarters and a light sprinkling of cheese. Cook 10 to 12 minutes or until bubbling hot.

Serves 6.

Stuffed Green Peppers
30 to 33 minutes

4 large green peppers, cut in half and core removed	⅛ tsp. pepper
	1 egg
	1 tsp. flour
1½ lbs. ground beef	½ cup hot water
1 cup cooked rice	1 cup tomato sauce
¼ cup chopped onion	
	1 tsp. sugar
¼ cup catsup	½ tsp. salt
1 tsp. salt	¼ tsp. pepper

Chicken Enchilada Casserole

Stuffed Green Peppers

Place 8 pepper halves, cut side up, on a large platter. Cover with plastic wrap. Cook 6 minutes. Turn cut side down and cook 6 minutes longer. Combine next 7 ingredients and stuff into green pepper halves in 7 x 11-inch utility dish. In 1 quart casserole dish, gradually combine water with flour, stirring to avoid lumping. Add remaining ingredients, stirring to combine. Cook 3 to 4 minutes.

Place 1 tablespoon of sauce over top of each stuffed pepper. Cover with plastic wrap. Cook 11 to 13 minutes. Pour remaining sauce over stuffed peppers. Cook 4 minutes.

Serves 8.

Hamburger Corn Casserole

Lazy Day Ham Casserole
16 to 17 minutes

8 oz. medium noodles	1 Tbs. chopped parsley, fresh or dried
2 cups diced cooked ham	1 tsp. salt
½ onion, chopped	½ tsp. pepper
1 clove garlic, minced	1 (4 oz.) can mushrooms, drained
2 Tbs. butter or margarine	1 (1 lb.) can whole kernel corn, drained
1 can (10½ oz.) cream of chicken soup, undiluted	1 cup grated cheddar cheese
½ cup milk	
2 Tbs. all-purpose flour	
1 (2 oz.) jar pimiento, drained and chopped	

Cook noodles in salted water, according to package directions, on top of range. While they are cooking, sauté ham, onion, and garlic with butter in a 3-quart glass casserole dish, 4 to 5 minutes. Add cooked and drained noodles and all remaining ingredients to ham mixture. Mix thoroughly; cover and cook 6 minutes, stir, then cook 6 minutes longer.

Serves 8.

Hamburger Corn Casserole
15 to 16 minutes

3 cups (8 to 10 oz.) macaroni rings	1 can chicken rice soup
1 lb. beef, ground round or chuck	1 can (#2) cream corn
1 green pepper, chopped	1 tsp. salt
1 medium onion	¼ tsp. pepper

Cook macaroni on range top, 8 to 10 minutes. Drain. Meanwhile, sauté meat, green pepper, and onion in 3-quart casserole dish. Cook 5 to 6 minutes. Add drained macaroni to meat mixture. Add soup, corn, salt, and pepper. Cook 10 minutes.

Serves 6 to 8.

Lasagne
31 to 37 minutes

8 oz. lasagne noodles	3 cups cottage or ricotta cheese
1 lb. ground beef or Italian sausage	½ cup grated Parmesan cheese
1 clove garlic, minced	2 Tbs. parsley flakes
1 Tbs. sweet basil	2 beaten eggs
1 tsp. salt	2 tsp. salt
1 (1 lb.) can tomatoes	½ tsp. pepper
2 (6 oz.) cans tomato paste	1 lb. mozzarella cheese, sliced thin or grated

Lasagne

of noodles, then layer of meat sauce, and top with mozzarella cheese. Bake, one dish at a time, 8 to 10 minutes, turning dish once. Let stand 10 minutes before cutting into squares and serving.

Use your blender for combining the sauce ingredients before adding to the cooked meat. This breaks up the garlic and tomato better. If your oven is large enough, cook the recipe in one 9 x 12 baking dish.

Serves 8 to 10.

Cook noodles in large amount of boiling salted water on top of the range until tender; drain and rinse. Break up meat in mixing bowl. Cook 5 to 7 minutes, stirring after 3 minutes. Drain excess fat. Add next 5 ingredients and cook, stirring occasionally, 10 minutes. Combine remaining ingredients except for mozzarella cheese. Divide evenly between 2 8-inch square baking dishes. Place layer of cooked noodles on bottom of each casserole, follow with layer of cottage cheese mixture, another layer

Up North Salmon Supper

22½ to 23½ minutes

2 cups (1 lb. can) pink or red salmon	1 cup grated cheddar cheese
1 (10 oz.) package frozen peas	3 Tbs. chopped green pepper
1½ cups cottage cheese	1 Tbs. chopped onion
1 egg, slightly beaten	2 Tbs. lemon juice
1 cup cracker crumbs	⅛ tsp. pepper
½ cup crushed rice cereal or cornflakes	Salt to taste
	Lemon Almond Butter Sauce

Drain salmon into a 2½-quart casserole dish; flake and set aside. Partially cook peas in salmon liquid, 4 minutes, stirring once. Add remaining ingredients, including salmon. Mix until well combined. Cover and cook 13 minutes, stirring every 5 minutes.

Lemon Almond Butter Sauce

½ cup blanched, slivered, almonds	3 to 4 Tbs. lemon juice
½ cup butter or margarine	

Toast almonds in microwave oven on a paper towel 3 to 4 minutes, stirring every minute. Place butter and lemon juice in a serving pitcher or dish, cover with paper towel and heat 2½ minutes. Add almonds. Pass sauce to spoon over casserole.

Serves 6.

Spam mit Sauerkraut und Äpfeln

Spam mit Sauerkraut und Äpfeln
5 to 7 minutes

1 (1 lb.) can
 sauerkraut,
 drained
2 cooking apples,
 sliced thin
½ cup firmly
 packed brown
 sugar

2 tsp. prepared
 mustard
1 tsp. water
1 (12 oz.) can
 Spam, sliced

Mix sauerkraut, apples, and half of sugar in a 2-quart casserole dish. Mix remaining sugar with mustard and water. Spread on both sides of the Spam slices. Arrange Spam slices in a cartwheel design on top of sauerkraut. Cook 5 to 7 minutes.
Serves 6.

Gourmet Casserole
16 to 21 minutes

1 lb. sausage
1 medium onion,
 chopped
1 medium green
 pepper, chopped
½ cup chopped
 celery
1 (6 oz.) package
 white and wild
 rice, cooked
1 can cream of
 chicken soup
1 can cream of
 mushroom soup

1 (2 oz.) can
 mushrooms,
 drained
1 (2 oz.) jar
 pimiento,
 chopped
1 cup grated sharp
 cheese

Cook sausage in 7 x 11-inch utility dish for 3 minutes, stir, cook 3 to 4 minutes longer. Add onion, green pepper, and celery. Cook 3 to 5 minutes. Drain off excess fat. Stir in rice, cooked as directed on package, soups, mushrooms, and pimiento. Bake 5 to 7 minutes. Top with cheese. Bake 2 minutes longer.

All white rice or all wild rice can be used in place of the combination.
Serves 8.

Macaroni Ring with Shrimp Filling
10 to 13 minutes

1 (12 oz.) package
 macaroni
1 (13 oz.) can
 evaporated
 milk
2 cups grated
 sharp cheese
3 eggs, beaten
½ cup fresh bread
 crumbs
1½ tsp. salt
½ tsp. pepper
¼ tsp. cayenne
 pepper
 (optional)

1 (4 oz.) jar
 pimientos,
 drained and
 chopped
1 (4 oz.) can
 sliced
 mushrooms,
 drained
1 (10½ oz.) can
 cream of
 mushroom soup
3 (4 to 5 oz.) cans
 shrimp or ¾ to
 1 lb. cooked
 fresh shrimp

Cook macaroni on top of conventional range as directed on package. Combine milk, cheese, eggs, bread crumbs, salt, and peppers in a large mixing bowl. Butter a 10-inch glass pie dish and place in the center a jar or glass that measures 3 inches across to form a ring mold. Sprinkle bottom of dish with half of the pimientos. Drain macaroni and toss with cheese mixture. Pack firmly into mold. Cook until set, 6 to 8 minutes.

Macaroni Ring with Shrimp Filling

Combine mushrooms, soup, shrimp, and remaining pimientos in a 2-quart casserole dish. Cook until hot, stirring a couple of times, 4 to 5 minutes. Invert macaroni ring onto large serving dish. Fill with shrimp mixture and serve hot.

Cover for reheating. Also may be frozen. Use your blender to prepare the bread crumbs and grate the cheese.

Serves 6 to 8.

Taco Casserole
23 to 25 minutes

1 (10 oz.) package mixed vegetables, frozen in butter sauce	1 (1¼ oz.) package taco seasoning
2 lbs. lean ground beef	1 cup water
½ cup chopped onion	5 cups corn chips
	1 (10 oz.) can enchilada sauce
	2 cups shredded cheddar cheese

Cook vegetables in 1-quart casserole until thawed, 3 minutes. Combine beef and onions in baking dish. Cook 7 minutes, stirring occasionally. Add taco seasoning and water; cover with plastic wrap and cook 5 minutes. Stir in mixed vegetables. Sprinkle 2 cups corn chips over the bottom of a greased 7 x 11-inch baking dish. Add half of the meat mixture, top with half of the enchilada sauce, and sprinkle with half of the cheese. Repeat next layer, ending with 1 cup corn chips. Cook 8 to 10 minutes.

Serves 6.

Tuna Soufflé
16 to 19 minutes

1 can cream of mushroom soup, undiluted	1 cup cooked rice
1 cup grated sharp cheese	1 (2 oz.) jar chopped pimiento
¼ tsp. dry mustard	2 Tbs. dried parsley
1 (6½ oz.) can tuna, drained and flaked	4 eggs, separated
	¼ tsp. cream of tartar

Combine soup, cheese, and mustard in 2½-quart bowl. Cook 2½ minutes, stirring after 1½ minutes. Add tuna, rice, pimiento, and parsley. Cook 1½ minutes.

Beat egg yolks until thick and lemon-colored, and gradually stir into tuna mixture. Beat egg whites until frothy, add cream of tartar, and beat until stiff, but not dry. Carefully fold in beaten whites, folding together thoroughly. Cook, covered with plastic wrap, 12 to 15 minutes, turning dish every 5 minutes. After cooking, let stand 5 minutes, covered, before serving.

Serves 4 to 6.

Noël Turkey Casserole
20 to 25 minutes

10 slices bread	4 eggs, beaten
2 cups cooked turkey, diced	1 cup mayonnaise
1 cup celery, diced	2 cups milk
1 small onion, finely chopped	1 can (10½ oz.) cream of mushroom soup
1 (4 oz.) can mushrooms, drained	¼ cup grated cheese

Butter bread on both sides. Put five slices of bread in bottom of 7 x 11-inch baking dish, cutting last slice to fit baking dish. Mix turkey, celery, onion, and mushrooms and sprinkle

Noël Turkey Casserole

over bread. Top with remaining five slices of bread. Mix eggs and mayonnaise until smooth, add milk, and pour mixture over bread. Cover and refrigerate overnight. Before baking, spread mushroom soup over mixture and top with cheese. Bake, uncovered, 20 to 25 minutes, turning after 10 minutes. Let stand 5 minutes before serving.

Serves 6 to 8.

California Casserole
16 to 20 minutes

2 lbs. fresh broccoli or 2 (10 oz.) packages frozen broccoli spears	¼ cup sherry Salt, celery salt, and pepper to taste
¼ cup cream or undiluted evaporated milk	2 (5 oz.) can boned chicken
1 (10½ oz.) can cream of chicken soup	2 hard-cooked eggs, sliced ¼ cup grated Parmesan cheese

Wash broccoli if fresh; trim off large leaves and ends of stalks. Split stems with a sharp knife so they will cook more quickly. Place in a 7 x 11-inch baking dish and cover with plastic wrap. Cook 10 to 12 minutes. Drain and set

Chinese Casserole

aside. Combine remaining ingredients except cheese. Pour over broccoli and sprinkle with cheese. Cook until bubbly, 6 to 8 minutes.

Serves 4 to 5.

Chinese Casserole
8 minutes

1 (8 oz.) can water chestnuts	⅔ cup water ½ cup chopped celery
1 (7 oz.) package frozen rice and peas with mushrooms	½ tsp. salt ½ tsp. soy sauce
1 (5½ oz.) can boned chicken or 1 cup cooked chicken	

Drain water chestnuts, reserving liquid; slice. Combine with remaining ingredients in a 1½-quart casserole dish. Add liquid from chestnuts. Cover. Cook 5 minutes, stir, cook 3 minutes longer. Let stand 5 minutes before serving.

Serves 4.

Rice Vegetable Soufflé
10½ to 14 minutes

¼ cup butter or margarine	1 Tbs. chopped pimiento
¼ cup flour	2 Tbs. minced green pepper
1 cup milk	
½ tsp. salt	
4 eggs, separated	
¾ cup cooked rice	
½ cup whole-kernel corn or other cooked vegetable	

Melt butter, 30 seconds to 1 minute. Blend in flour. Gradually add milk. Cook until smooth and thickened, 2 to 3 minutes, stirring after each minute. Add salt and slightly beaten egg yolks. Fold in rice and vegetables. Beat egg whites until stiff but not dry. Fold into rice mixture. Pour into ungreased 2-quart casserole and cook 8 to 10 minutes. Serve hot.

Serves 4.

9
Vegetables

Your microwave oven is perfect for cooking fresh, canned, and frozen vegetables. They will have better flavor and color, as well as retaining more nutrients. During cooking, most vegetables should be covered. Exceptions are potatoes or squash that are cooked with the skins on. If plastic wrap is used, remove it carefully, since steam accumulates during cooking.

Remove vegetables while slightly underdone; they will continue to cook outside the oven. Watch cooking times carefully so as not to overcook. Stir halfway through cooking time, and test during last minutes for doneness. Except for starchy vegetables, most will require little or no water. Potatoes in skins could be cooked on a paper towel. Arrange in a circle about an inch apart, and turn once during cooking.

Frozen vegetables can be cooked in paper cartons or plastic cooking pouches. Pierce pouch on top to let steam escape. Place vegetables icy side up when cooking in dish. Specific instructions for cooking frozen foods by microwave are being incorporated onto packaging by frozen food companies. Look for them and follow them when cooking.

Canned vegetables can be drained and heated quickly in a covered casserole dish. Butter and seasonings can be added before heating, garnishes afterward. Sauces or cheese can be added and dish reheated. For variety, try lima beans with corn or other combinations.

Cooking Chart Fresh Vegetables

Vegetable	Amount	Dish	Add	Stir	Time
Artichokes	1	2 qt. covered			4– 4½ minutes
	2	or wax paper			6– 7 minutes
	3				8– 9 minutes
	4				10–11 minutes
Asparagus	15	1½ qt. covered or 1½ qt. oblong, covered	½ cup water or butter		4–4½ minutes
	30	2 qt. covered	Same	once	9–10 minutes

Beans, green or wax	1 lb.	1½ qt. covered	⅓ cup water or butter	once	10–12 minutes
	2 lbs.	2 qt. covered	same	once	14–16 minutes
Lima Beans	1 lb.	1 qt. covered	½ cup water	once	6–8 minutes
	2 lbs.	1½ qt. covered	same	once	9–12 minutes
Beets, whole	4 medium	2 qt. covered	cover with water	once	15–17 minutes
Broccoli	1½ lbs. stalks split	1½ qt. covered	¼ cup water or butter	once	7–9 minutes
Brussels sprouts	½ lb.	1 qt. covered	2 Tbs. water or butter		4–5 minutes
Cabbage	1 small head, chopped or shredded	1½ qt. covered	2 Tbs. water or butter	once	7–9 minutes
	1 large head, chopped or shredded	2 qt. covered	same	once	10–13 minutes
Carrots	4, cut in strips or sliced	1 qt. covered	2 Tbs. water or butter		7–9 minutes
	8, cut in strips or sliced	1½ qt. covered	same	once	10–12 minutes
	6 whole	1½ qt. covered	same	once	10–12 minutes
Cauliflower	1 medium, in flowerets	1½ qt. covered	2 Tbs. water or butter		6–7 minutes
	1 medium, whole	same	same		7–8 minutes
Celery	4 cups sliced	1½ qt. covered	2 Tbs. water or butter		9–10 minutes
Corn, cut from cob	1½ cups	1 qt. covered	2 Tbs. water or butter		5–6 minutes
	3 cups	same	same	once	6–8 minutes
Corn on cob	1 ear	wrap in wax paper or plastic wrap	butter if desired		2–3 minutes
	2 ears	same	same		4– 5 minutes
	3 ears	same	same		5– 6 minutes
	4 ears	same	same		7– 8 minutes
	6 ears	same	same		9–10 minutes

Vegetable	Amount	Dish	Add	Stir	Time
Onions, cut in quarters	2 large or 8 small	1 qt. covered	none		7–9 minutes
	4 large	1½ qt. covered	none		9–10 minutes
Parsnips, cut in quarters	4 medium	1½ qt. covered	½ cup water		7–9 minutes
	8 medium	2 qt. covered	same	once	10–12 minutes
Peas, green, shelled	2 lbs.	1 qt. covered	2 Tbs. water or butter	once	7–9 minutes
	3 lbs.	1½ qt. covered	same	once	10–11 minutes
Pea pods	1 lb.	1 qt. covered	2 Tbs. water or butter	once	5–6 minutes
Potatoes, baked	1 medium 2 medium 3 medium 4 medium 5 medium 6 medium 7 medium 8 medium	Prick skin, lay on paper towel. 1" space between each potato			4– 6 minutes 6– 8 minutes 9–10 minutes 11–12 minutes 13–14 minutes 15–16 minutes 18–20 minutes 21–23 minutes
Potatoes, boiled, quartered	4 medium	1½ qt. covered	cover with water		8–10 minutes
	6 medium	2 qt. covered	same		12–14 minutes
Potatoes, buttered	4 medium, sliced thin	1½ qt. shallow utility dish	3 Tbs. butter	once	8–10 minutes
	6 medium, sliced thin	2 qt. shallow utility dish	4 Tbs. butter	once	12–15 minutes
Potatoes, sweet or yams, whole	1 medium 2 medium 4 medium 6 medium	cut off both ends of potato, lay on paper towel. 1" space between each potato			3–4 minutes 5–6 minutes 7–8 minutes 9–10 minutes
Spinach	½ lb.	2 qt. covered	water that clings when washed		4–5 minutes
	1 lb.	same			5–7 minutes
Squash, Hubbard	2 lbs., peeled and cubed	1½ qt. covered	¼ cup water or butter	once	6–8 minutes
Squash, acorn or butternut, whole	1 medium	lay on paper towel			5–7 minutes
	2 medium				10–12 minutes

Squash, zucchini, sliced	2 cups	1 qt. covered	2 Tbs. water or butter	once	4–5 minutes
	4 cups	1½ qt. covered	same	once	5–7 minutes
Turnips, cut in eighths	4 medium	1½ qt. covered	¼ cup water		10–12 minutes
	8 medium	2 qt. covered	same	once	12–15 minutes

Acorn Squash

Artichokes

Acorn Squash
16 to 17 minutes

3 acorn squash	¼ cup chopped walnuts
2 cups canned applesauce	
⅓ cup brown sugar	2 Tbs. butter or margarine
1 Tbs. lemon juice	
⅓ cup seedless raisins	

Wash squash, pierce with a fork, and place in a large baking dish. Cook 9 minutes, turn over, and cook 7 to 8 minutes. Cut squash open and spoon out pulp and seeds. Combine remaining ingredients except butter and fill center of squash. Dot with butter. Cook 6 to 8 minutes or until center mixture is well heated.

Serves 6.

Artichokes
12 to 15 minutes

2 medium globe artichokes	1 cup boiling water

Clean artichokes under cold running water. Cut off about 1 inch of the top, trim stem. Pull off loose leaves around bottom. With scissors snip off sharp leaf tips if desired, and brush the cut edges with lemon juice to prevent darkening.

Place artichokes in 3-quart casserole and cover tightly with plastic wrap, then with glass cover. (If casserole does not have a lid use two coverings of plastic wrap.) Cook 12 to 15 minutes. Let stand 10 minutes. Serve with blender hollandaise, packaged hollandaise sauce, melted butter, or mayonnaise.

Serves 2 to 4.

Asparagus with Oil and Lemon

Asparagus with Oil and Lemon
4¾ to 5¼ minutes

¾ lb. (15 stalks) fresh asparagus	¼ tsp. salt
¼ cup olive oil	⅛ tsp. pepper
2 tsp. chopped parsley	

Wash asparagus and peel lower portion. Place in 10 x 6-inch oblong baking dish, alternating blossom end. Cover with plastic wrap and cook 4 to 4½ minutes. Combine remaining ingredients in a 1-cup measurer. Heat 45 seconds. Pour over asparagus.
Serves 4.

Stuffed Avocados

Stuffed Avocados
2 to 3 minutes

3 large ripe avocados	¼ cup mayonnaise
Lemon juice	Lettuce
2 (6 oz.) cans boned chicken	Cherry tomatoes
1 cup celery, chopped	6 hard-cooked eggs, sliced
	Black olives

Peel and cut avocados in half lengthwise. Brush cut side with lemon juice. Mix together chicken, celery, and mayonnaise. Pile filling into center of avocado. Place in shallow baking dish and heat 2 to 3 minutes, or until hot. Serve on bed of lettuce. Garnish with cherry tomatoes, egg slices, and olives.
Serves 6.

Baked Beans

Baked Beans
9 to 11 minutes

1 (No. 2½) can pork and beans, drained	2 Tbs. bacon drippings
2 Tbs. brown sugar	1 Tbs. Worcestershire sauce
2 Tbs. molasses	2 Tbs. catsup
1 medium onion, diced fine	

Combine all ingredients in 1½ quart casserole dish. Cook 9 to 11 minutes. Top with one of the following. Put topping on beans for the last 1 to 2 minutes of cooking time.

Shredded sharp cheese
Toasted almonds, slivered and chopped
Chopped raw apple
Chopped dill pickle
Crumbled bacon
Canned peach slices
Pineapple chunks or tidbits
Apricot halves
Raisins
Serves 4.

Buttered Beets
17 to 19½ minutes

5 to 6 medium size fresh beets	2 Tbs. butter or margarine
½ to ¾ cup water	1 Tbs. lemon juice or vinegar
¼ tsp. salt	

Wash beets. Cut off tops, leaving about 1 inch of the tops attached to the beets. Place unpeeled beets in a 2-quart casserole, cover with water, and add salt. Cover casserole. Cook 16 to 18 minutes. Cool slightly and slip off the skins, stems, and roots by rubbing with the fingers. Serve whole, sliced, diced, or cut into shreds. Add butter and lemon juice. Heat thoroughly, 1 to 1½ minutes.
Serves 4.

Broccoli Mushroom Scallop
21 to 23 minutes

1½ lbs. fresh broccoli or 1 package frozen broccoli	1 tsp. grated onion
	2 Tbs. flour
2 Tbs. butter or margarine	¼ tsp. salt
	⅛ tsp. pepper
1 cup sliced fresh mushrooms or 1 (4 oz.) can sliced mushrooms, drained	1 cup milk
	¾ to 1 cup grated sharp cheese
	Paprika

Wash broccoli and split stalks in 3 to 4 places, then cut into 2-inch pieces. Cook in 2½-quart covered casserole 8 to 9 minutes. Combine butter, mushrooms, and onion in small bowl. Cook 3 minutes, stirring once.

Blend in flour and seasonings. Cook 3 minutes, stirring once. Slowly pour in milk, stirring until mixture is smooth. Cook 3 minutes, stirring once. Pour hot mushroom sauce over cooked broccoli. Sprinkle with cheese and paprika. Cook 4 to 5 minutes.
Serves 6.

Dilled Brussels Sprouts
14 to 18 minutes

2 packages frozen brussels sprouts	1 cup sour cream
	1 tsp. salt
6 strips bacon	½ tsp. dillweed
½ cup minced onion	¼ tsp. Tabasco sauce

Buttered Beets

Broccoli Mushroom Scallop

Cook brussels sprouts in a 2½-quart covered casserole dish 8 to 10 minutes. Drain if necessary. Fry bacon until crisp in a flat dish with one layer of paper toweling, 4 to 6 minutes. Drain and crumble. Remove paper towel from drippings to sauté onion, 2 minutes. Drain off excess fat. Blend onion, bacon, salt, dillweed and Tabasco sauce with sour cream. Pour over sprouts, sprinkle with paprika. Serve immediately. To reheat, cook about 1 minute or until warmed.

Other vegetables can be prepared with this basic sauce.

Serves 4 to 6.

Red Cabbage with Wine
13 to 15 minutes

2 Tbs. bacon fat or vegetable oil	1 tart apple, unpeeled and diced
1 medium onion, chopped	2 Tbs. brown sugar
1 medium red cabbage, shredded	1 Tbs. wine vinegar
1 cup red wine	Salt and pepper to taste

Place bacon fat and onion in a 3-quart casserole dish. Cook 2 minutes. Add cabbage, stir, cover, and cook 4 minutes. Add all remaining ingredients. Cover and cook 7 to 9 minutes. Do not overcook. Serve with duck, turkey, goose, or any kind of pork.

Serves 4 to 6.

Candied Carrots
11¾ to 12 minutes

18 tiny or 4 large carrots, cut in strips	½ cup sugar
	1 tsp. salt
	⅓ tsp. cinnamon
⅓ cup butter	1 Tbs. water

Scrape, cut, and arrange carrots in 8-inch square dish. Place remaining ingredients in small bowl and cook 45 seconds to 1 minute. Pour over carrots. Cover and cook 7 minutes, stirring once; baste, then cook 4 minutes longer.

Serves 4.

Almond-buttered Cauliflower
10 to 12 minutes

1 medium head cauliflower	½ cup butter or margarine
⅓ cup toasted almonds	1 tsp. lemon juice
	Parsley

Trim leaves but leave cauliflower whole. Hollow out most of the center core. Place cauliflower, stem side down, in 3-quart casserole dish. Cover with plastic wrap and cook 8 to 9 minutes. Toast almonds in microwave, 2 to 3 minutes. Melt butter with lemon juice; add toasted almonds. Place cauliflower on serving dish, pour almond butter over top of cauliflower. Garnish with parsley.

May also be served with a cheese sauce.

Serves 6.

Red Cabbage with Wine

Almond-buttered Cauliflower

Scalloped Celery
18 to 19 minutes

5 cups celery, cut into ¼-inch slices	½ cup milk
¾ cup water	¼ tsp. dry mustard
1 tsp. salt	1 cup herb seasoned bread dressing
1 (10½ oz.) can cream of chicken soup	2 Tbs. butter or margarine

Place celery, water, and salt in 2-quart covered casserole. Cook 11 to 12 minutes, stirring once. Let stand, covered, for 2 minutes. Drain. Mix soup, milk, and dry mustard with cooked celery. Cook 4 minutes. Stir. Top with seasoned bread dressing dotted with butter. Cook 3 minutes.
Serves 6.

Chinese Vegetable Trio
6 to 7 minutes

6 green onions with 2 inches of tops, chopped	8 stalks celery, sliced diagonally
½ lb. medium fresh mushrooms, sliced	2 Tbs. butter or margarine
	1 Tbs. soy sauce

Place vegetables in a 2½-quart casserole. Dot with butter and sprinkle with soy sauce. Cover and cook until tender and crisp, 6 to 7 minutes.
Serves 6.

Oriental Cucumbers

Corn on the Cob
8 to 10 minutes

4 ears fresh corn
Plastic wrap

Remove husks and silk from fresh corn. Rinse. Roll each ear individually in a piece of plastic wrap, leaving the ends open. Place corn in oven and cook 4 to 5 minutes. Turn corn, rotating outside ears to center of oven. Cook 4 to 5 minutes longer.

Corn Butter

Soften ½ cup butter and blend with any of the following:

½ to 1 tsp. chili powder	½ tsp. ground dill seed
1 tsp. curry powder	
1 tsp. ground oregano	

Serves 4.

Oriental Cucumbers
5½ to 5¾ minutes

3 medium cucumbers	½ tsp. salt
2 Tbs. butter or margarine	¼ tsp. pepper

Pare cucumbers, leaving a strip of peel on each one. Cut into quarters lengthwise. Scoop out any large seeds, if desired. Melt butter in 1½-quart casserole, 30 to 45 seconds. Add cucumbers and toss to coat with butter. Cover and cook 5 minutes. Add salt and pepper. Can be chilled and served as a salad on a bed of lettuce leaves.
Serves 6.

Savory Green Beans
8 to 10 minutes

2 (10 oz.) packages French cut green beans	¼ tsp. thyme
	¼ tsp. savory
¼ cup butter or margarine	

Combine all ingredients in a 1½-quart casserole. Cover and cook 8 to 10 minutes.
Serves 6.

Mushrooms Romanoff
6½ to 7½ minutes

⅓ cup butter or margarine
1 lb. whole mushrooms, washed and trimmed
½ tsp. salt
½ tsp. coarse ground pepper
1 Tbs. lemon juice
1 tsp. dried dill
⅛ tsp. nutmeg
1 cup sour cream, at room temperature

Melt butter in a 2½-quart casserole, 35 seconds. Add whole mushrooms, stirring so each mushroom is covered with melted butter. Cover. Cook 2 minutes, stir, cook 2 minutes longer. Add remaining ingredients, stirring until sour cream is well blended. Cover. Heat thoroughly, 2 to 3 minutes.
Serves 6.

Pea Pods with Water Chestnuts

Creamed Onions with Walnuts
14 to 17 minutes

6 large onions
⅓ cup butter or margarine
2 Tbs. flour
1 cup milk
½ tsp. salt
Pepper to taste
½ cup chopped walnuts

Peel onions and cut in quarters. Place in 1½-quart casserole dish. Add butter. Cover and cook until tender, 12 to 14 minutes, stirring once. Sprinkle flour over onions and stir carefully. Add milk gradually, stirring all the time. Cook until thick, 2 to 3 minutes, stirring every 30 seconds. Add salt, pepper, and nuts. Stir gently.

Can be prepared ahead, refrigerated, and reheated. Add nuts just before serving.
Serves 6.

French Parsnips
8½ to 9½ minutes

1 lb. parsnips, peeled and quartered
2 Tbs. butter or margarine
2 Tbs. brown sugar
¼ tsp. salt
Chopped parsley or mint

Place parsnips in an 8-inch round baking dish. Cover and cook 6 to 7 minutes, stirring once. Add remaining ingredients. Heat 2½ minutes.

To prevent discoloration, cook parsnips immediately after peeling.
Serves 4 to 6.

Pea Pods with Water Chestnuts
4 to 5 minutes

2 (7 oz.) packages frozen snow pea pods
1 (5 oz.) can water chestnuts
½ tsp. sugar
1 Tbs. soy sauce
1 Tbs. salad oil

In a 1½-quart casserole combine all ingredients. Cover and cook 4 to 5 minutes.
Serves 6.

Holiday Peas and Mushrooms
7 minutes

¼ lb. fresh mushrooms	¼ tsp. sugar
3 Tbs. butter	1 jar (2 oz.) pimiento, chopped
1 package (10 oz.) frozen peas	

Cook mushrooms and butter in a small dish, 2 minutes. Place peas, sugar, and pimiento in a 1-quart casserole. Cook, covered, 4½ minutes. Stir in mushrooms and butter. Cover and heat 1 minute.

Serves 6.

Cheese-stuffed Potatoes
10 to 12 minutes

4 medium baking potatoes	1 tsp. evaporated milk
½ glass pimiento cream cheese	Chopped parsley

Wash and dry potatoes. With paring knife or long fork, pierce completely through largest part of each potato. Place in circle in oven with space between each potato. Cook 10 to 12 minutes. Mash cheese with milk, form into walnut-size balls. When potatoes are done, let them stand for about 5 minutes. Cut an X in top of each potato and squeeze open by pressing fingers toward the opening. Top with cheese balls and sprinkle with parsley.

Serves 4.

Potatoes Romanoff
13 to 16 minutes

5 cups frozen hash-brown cut potatoes	2 tsp. salt
2 cups creamed cottage cheese	1 small clove garlic, minced
1 cup dairy sour cream	½ cup grated cheddar cheese
¼ cup minced green onion	Paprika

Place frozen potatoes in 3-quart casserole dish. Cover. Cook 6 to 7 minutes, stirring once. Combine cottage cheese, sour cream, green onion, salt, and garlic with cooked potatoes. Cook 4 to 5 minutes stirring every 2 minutes. Sprinkle with grated cheese and paprika. Cook 3 to 4 minutes.

Serves 8.

New Potatoes with Mint
13½ to 16¾ minutes

6 new potatoes	2 Tbs. lemon juice
½ cup water	2 tsp. fresh mint, chopped
½ cup butter or margarine	

Wash potatoes. Pare a strip about 1 inch wide around center of each potato. Place in 2-quart casserole dish; add water. Cover with plastic wrap or glass cover. Cook 13 to 16 minutes. Drain well. Place butter, lemon juice, and mint in glass measuring cup. Heat until butter

Cheese-stuffed Potatoes

Potatoes Romanoff

melts (30 to 45 seconds). Pour over potatoes; toss until potatoes are well coated. Garnish with mint sprigs.

Serves 6.

German Fried Potatoes
14 minutes

4 potatoes, sliced thin (3 cups)	1 Tbs. caraway seeds
¼ cup butter or margarine	Salt and pepper

Place potato slices in 7 x 11-inch utility dish. Dot with butter. Sprinkle caraway seeds over top. Salt and pepper to taste. Cover dish with waxed paper. Cook 8 minutes, stirring after 4 minutes. Remove waxed paper and continue cooking 6 minutes longer, stirring after each 2 minutes.

Serves 4 to 6.

Quick Orange Rice
2 to 3 minutes

1⅓ cups packaged precooked rice	1 Tbs. grated orange rind
1⅓ cups water	½ cup chopped pecans
1½ Tbs. butter	
½ tsp. salt	

Spinach Pudding

Place all ingredients except pecans in 2-quart casserole dish. Cover and cook just until water boils, 2 to 3 minutes. Allow to stand covered 5 minutes. Stir in pecans.

Pecans can be toasted for extra flavor. Dried orange rind or orange bits can be substituted.

Serves 4.

Spinach Pudding
23 to 24 minutes

2 (10 oz.) packages frozen chopped spinach	⅓ cup grated Parmesan cheese
2 cups cottage cheese	2 eggs
1 tsp. salt	Parmesan cheese

Cook spinach in microwave oven in covered dish 8 to 9 minutes, stirring after 5 minutes. Drain. Mix together with cottage cheese, salt, Parmesan cheese, and eggs until well blended. Pour into a greased 1½-quart casserole. Bake 15 minutes, turning every 5 minutes. Sprinkle with Parmesan cheese.

Spinach may be cooked in package. Split package so steam can escape, and turn package once during cooking.

Serves 8.

Sweet Potato Orange Cups
8 minutes

3 oranges, halved	¼ cup packed brown sugar
1 (No. 2½) can sweet potatoes or yams	1 tsp. salt
	1 tsp. cinnamon
3 Tbs. melted butter or margarine	2 Tbs. brown sugar

Remove pulp from orange halves, chop fine, and reserve (should make about 2 cups). Drain sweet potatoes well and mash. Combine with orange pulp, butter, brown sugar, and salt. Mix well. Spoon potato mixture into orange cups. Combine cinnamon and brown sugar. Sprinkle about 1 teaspoon over each cup. Bake 8 minutes, turning dish once.

If you prefer, use fresh sweet potatoes, baked in the microwave oven.

Serves 6.

Herbed Baked Tomatoes
4½ to 4¾ minutes

3 large tomatoes
½ cup butter or margarine
1 Tbs. chopped fresh parsley
¼ tsp. thyme
¼ tsp. rosemary, crushed
¼ tsp. tarragon
Parsley sprigs
Grated sharp or Parmesan cheese (optional)

Slice tomatoes in half horizontally. Melt butter, 30 to 45 seconds. Add herbs. Place tomatoes in buttered 7 x 11-inch utility dish. Pour butter mixture over tomatoes. Bake 4 minutes. Garnish each tomato half with small sprig of parsley. Sprinkle with cheese if desired.
Serves 6.

Herbed Baked Tomatoes

Oriental Tomato Bake
9 to 10 minutes

2 Tbs. butter
½ cup chopped onion
4 medium unpared zucchini squash, cut in quarters
3 medium tomatoes, cut in wedges
Dash of freshly ground pepper
1 (4 oz.) can broiled mushrooms, drained
¼ tsp. salt
¼ tsp. curry powder
¼ tsp. ground ginger

Combine butter, onion, and zucchini in a 2-quart casserole. Cover and cook 5 minutes. Add all remaining ingredients, stir, cover, and cook 4 to 5 minutes.
Serves 6.

Winter Squash with Dill and Sour Cream
10 to 12 minutes

2 lbs. banana or hubbard squash
1 tsp. salt
½ cup dairy sour cream
½ tsp. dillweed
1 Tbs. instant onions, toasted
¼ tsp. pepper

Oriental Tomato Bake

Pare off tough rind and cut squash into one-inch cubes. Place in 1½-quart casserole dish. Cover and cook, stirring after half the cooking time, 10 to 12 minutes. Drain liquid and toss gently with salt, sour cream, dillweed, and onion. Sprinkle with pepper. Cover until ready to serve.
Serves 6.

Candied Yams
9 to 12 minutes

2 (1 lb. 2 oz.) cans yams, drained
½ cup pecans, chopped
¼ cup butter or margarine
¾ cup brown sugar
½ cup apricot nectar

Arrange yams in 2-quart greased casserole dish. Press pecans into top of yams. Combine butter, sugar, and nectar in 1-quart bowl or measurer. Cook until syrupy, stirring once, 3 to 5 minutes. Pour syrup over yams and bake uncovered, basting occasionally, 6 to 7 minutes.

If recipe is prepared and refrigerated ahead of time, allow 2 to 3 more minutes for cooking. Serves 8 to 10.

Chinese Zucchini
6½ to 8 minutes

2 tsp. sugar
2 tsp. cornstarch
1 Tbs. soy sauce
⅓ cup water
2 cloves garlic, minced
2 Tbs. cooking oil
½ tsp. salt
3 medium zucchini, cut in ½-inch slices
1 medium onion, cut in ¼-inch rounds

Mix sugar, cornstarch, soy sauce, and water and let stand. Cook garlic in oil with salt in a 10-inch pie dish or glass skillet, 2 minutes. Add zucchini and onions. Cook, covered, 3 to 4 minutes. Add soy mixture to zucchini. Stir well. Cover and cook 1½ to 2 minutes.
Serves 6.

Vegetable Casserole
21 to 24 minutes

1 (10 oz.) package frozen cut green beans
2 (10 oz.) packages frozen whole-kernel corn
½ cup water
½ cup butter or margarine
1 clove garlic, crushed
2 cups sliced onion
3 large tomatoes, coarsely chopped
2 Tbs. chopped parsley
1 tsp. salt
½ tsp. dried thyme leaves
¼ tsp. pepper

In 2-quart casserole combine beans, corn, and water. Cover and cook 10 to 12 minutes; set aside. Combine butter, garlic, and onion in a 1-quart dish. Cook 2 minutes. Add tomatoes, parsley, salt, thyme, and pepper. Cover and cook 3 minutes. In a 2½-quart casserole, arrange corn mixture in layers alternately with tomato mixture. Cook, covered, 6 to 7 minutes or until heated through.

Serves 6 to 8.

Vegetable Casserole

10
Sauces and Condiments

Sauces

Watch sauces carefully to avoid boilovers; stir frequently to avoid lumps. Use a wooden spoon that may be left in the dish for easy stirring. Cook uncovered unless otherwise specified in recipe.

Sauce cooked in a gravy boat or small pitcher is easy to serve and easy to reheat. Try the many packaged sauces; cook them in a 1-quart measurer. Milk sauces should be watched closely. Sauces continue to cook after being taken out of the oven, so never overcook.

Béchamel Sauce
7 minutes

2 Tbs. butter or margarine	2 Tbs. flour
½ cup chopped onion	2 Tbs. cream
1 cup water	Salt and pepper
2 chicken bouillon cubes	½ cup Parmesan cheese

Combine butter and onion in a small bowl. Combine water with bouillon cubes in a 1-cup glass measuring cup. Place both containers in oven at the same time. Cook 3½ minutes. Add flour to butter-onion mixture. Stir until smooth. Gradually pour in hot chicken bouillon, stirring constantly. Stir in cream, salt, and pepper. Cook 3½ minutes, stirring every minute. Add cheese.
Makes 1½ cups.

Cherry Sauce
4 to 5½ minutes

1 (1 lb.) can pitted red sour cherries	1 Tbs. butter
Water	Pinch of salt
½ cup sugar	Red food coloring
2 Tbs. cornstarch	

Drain cherries and set aside. Add enough water to juice to make 1 cup. Place juice in 1-quart dish. Add remaining ingredients. Cook until thick, 3 to 4 minutes, stirring occasionally. Add cherries and heat 1 to 1½ minutes. Serve with chicken or ham.

Makes 2 cups.

Deviled Ham Sauce
3 to 4 minutes

2 Tbs. butter or margarine	1 cup milk
2 Tbs. flour	1 (2¼ oz.) can deviled ham
½ tsp. salt	

Melt butter in 1-quart casserole dish; add flour and salt and blend to a smooth paste. Add milk gradually, stirring constantly. Cook uncovered 1 minute, stir; cook 1½ to 2 minutes longer, stirring every 30 seconds. Add deviled ham and blend well. Cook ½ to 1 minute or until hot. Use with broccoli or asparagus.

Makes 1¼ cups.

Golden Ham Sauce
1½ to 2 minutes

½ cup golden seedless raisins	1 Tbs. cornstarch
¼ cup brown sugar	1 tsp. dry mustard
1⅓ cups pineapple juice	

In a 1-quart casserole dish, combine all ingredients. Cook until sauce thickens and is clear, 1½ to 2 minutes, stirring every 30 seconds. Serve hot.

Makes 1½ cups.

Lemon Butter Sauce
¾ to 1¼ minutes

½ cup butter	1 Tbs. chopped parsley (optional)
2 Tbs. lemon juice	
Salt and pepper to taste	

Place all ingredients except parsley in 1-pint measuring cup. Heat ¾ to 1¼ minutes. Stir. Add parsley. Use with vegetables or fish.

Makes ½ cup.

Marinara Sauce
18 to 20 minutes

¼ cup olive oil	2 tsp. parsley
2 cups finely chopped onion	4 Tbs. butter
½ cup finely chopped carrot	1 tsp. oregano
2 cloves garlic, finely chopped	1 Tbs. fresh basil
4 cups canned Italian plum tomatoes, undrained	1 tsp. salt
	¼ tsp. pepper

Combine oil, onion, carrot, and garlic in 2½-quart ceramic skillet. Cook 8 minutes. Add remaining ingredients; cover and cook 10 to 12 minutes. Serve hot with any pasta.

Add ¼ cup finely grated Romano cheese during last few minutes of cooking time. Or add ½ cup dry red wine in place of ½ cup of tomato liquid.

Makes 6 cups.

Mexican Sauce
7 to 10 minutes

2 Tbs. butter or bacon drippings	½ tsp. Kitchen Bouquet
1½ Tbs. minced onion	½ cup tomato catsup
1½ Tbs. minced green pepper	¼ tsp. celery seed
2 Tbs. flour	Salt and pepper to taste
1 cup hot water	Paprika
1 bouillon cube	

In 1-quart glass casserole, combine butter or bacon drippings with onion and green pepper. Cook covered until vegetables are limp, 2 to 3 minutes. Stir in flour until well blended. Dissolve bouillon cube in water. Add slowly to casserole, stirring constantly. Add Kitchen Bouquet, catsup, and celery seed. Bring to a boil, 1 minute. Cook 4 to 6 minutes, stirring after 1 minute, then every 30 seconds. Add salt, pepper, and paprika to taste. Stir well. Serve over scrambled eggs.

Makes 1½ cups.

Mint Sauce
1 to 2 minutes

1 cup hot cider vinegar
¼ cup finely chopped fresh mint
¼ cup sugar
Dash of salt

Put vinegar in 2-cup glass measuring cup. Heat 1 to 2 minutes. Stir in mint, sugar and salt; stir until sugar dissolves. Serve with lamb.

Makes 1 cup.

Mushroom Barbecue Sauce
6 to 9 minutes

1 can (5¾ oz.) mushroom steak sauce
2 packages onion soup mix
1 cup catsup
2 Tbs. brown sugar
1 Tbs. salad oil
1 Tbs. mustard
1 Tbs. Worcestershire sauce
⅛ tsp. hot pepper sauce

Combine all ingredients in a 1-quart mixing bowl; stir well. Cook 6 to 9 minutes, stirring occasionally. Serve over chicken, pork chops, or steaks.

Makes 2 cups.

Orange Spicy Glaze
1½ to 2 minutes

¼ cup orange marmalade
¼ cup honey
2 Tbs. water
1 Tbs. lemon juice
1 tsp. bottled browning sauce
⅛ tsp. salt
⅛ tsp. ground ginger
⅛ tsp. cinnamon

Smoky Barbecue Sauce

Combine all ingredients. Cook 1½ to 2 minutes. Use to brush on chicken or ham.

Makes ⅔ cup.

Smoky Barbecue Sauce
13 to 15 minutes

¼ cup brown sugar
¼ cup cider vinegar
⅔ cup catsup
⅓ cup water
2 Tbs. soy sauce
1 Tbs. prepared mustard
1 medium onion, chopped fine
6 very thin lemon slices
¼ cup salad oil
¼ tsp. coarsely ground pepper
1½ tsp. salt
2 tsp. liquid smoke

Mix all ingredients thoroughly in a 2-quart casserole dish. Cook until sauce begins to thicken, 5 minutes. Stir. Cook 8 to 10 minutes longer, stirring every 3 minutes. Sauce will thicken more as it cools. Store in refrigerator. Use on all meat, especially lamb.

Makes 2½ cups.

Spanish Spaghetti Sauce
23 to 28 minutes

2 Tbs. olive oil
1 medium onion, chopped fine
1 clove garlic, minced
½ cup parsley, chopped
1 (1 lb. 12 oz.) can peeled tomatoes

1 (6 oz.) can tomato paste
½ cup water
2 tsp. sugar
¼ tsp. salt
⅛ tsp. pepper
2 cups diced cooked turkey or chicken

Combine oil, onion, and garlic in 3-quart casserole dish. Cook 3 minutes, stirring occasionally. Add all other ingredients except turkey or chicken. Stir and break up larger pieces of tomato. Cover and cook 20 to 25 minutes, stirring occasionally. Stir in turkey or chicken; cover and let stand 5 to 10 minutes. Serve over spaghetti.

Canned turkey or chicken can be substituted, or canned tuna.

Makes 6 cups.

Spanish Spaghetti Sauce

White Sauce
2¾ minutes

2 Tbs. butter or margarine
2 Tbs. flour
1½ cups milk
½ tsp. salt

Melt butter, 15 to 20 seconds. Stir in flour. Gradually add milk, stirring constantly. Cook 1 minute, stir, then 1½ minutes, stirring every 30 seconds.

Add 1 to 2 cups grated cheese for a rich cheese sauce.

Makes 1½ cups.

Condiments

Currant Relish
6 to 9 minutes

1 (11 oz.) box currants
1 (1 lb.) can fruit cocktail, undrained
⅓ cup lemon juice
¼ cup sugar
½ tsp. cinnamon
¼ tsp. cloves

Dash of salt
1 tsp. grated orange rind, fresh or dried
1 tsp. grated lemon rind, fresh or dried
1 Tbs. quick-cooking tapioca

Combine currants and fruit in a 2-quart casserole dish. Add lemon juice. Mix sugar, spices, peel, and tapioca. Add to fruit and mix well. Bring to a boil, 6 to 9 minutes. Chill. Serve with roast turkey or chicken.

Makes 3 cups.

Mushroom Relish
6 to 7 minutes

2 (3 oz.) cans chopped broiled mushrooms
¼ cup cider vinegar
1 cup pared chopped apples

¼ cup finely chopped onions
¼ cup raisins
½ tsp. pickling spices
¼ cup brown sugar

Mushroom Relish

Walnut Cranberry Relish

In 1-quart mixing bowl combine mushroom liquid, vinegar, apples, onions, raisins, and pickling spices. Cover with plastic wrap. Cook 3 minutes. Add sugar and mushrooms and mix well. Cover. Cook 3 to 4 minutes. Refrigerate until ready to serve.

Makes 1¾ cups.

Walnut Cranberry Relish
14 to 16 minutes

1 lb. fresh cranberries, mashed	1 Tbs. butter or margarine
1½ cups sugar	1 cup orange marmalade
1 cup coarsely chopped walnuts	3 Tbs. lemon juice

Combine cranberries and sugar in a 7 x 11-inch utility dish. Stir to dissolve sugar. Cover with plastic wrap. Cook 11 to 13 minutes, stirring every 5 minutes. Place nuts in small bowl with butter or margarine. Heat 3 minutes. Mix nuts with cooked cranberries. Add marmalade and lemon juice. Mix well. Refrigerate, covered, at least 6 hours. Serve with turkey, chicken, or beef.

Makes 4 cups.

Mint Jelly
11 to 14 minutes

1½ cups fresh mint, packed	3¼ cups sugar
3 cups water	Green food coloring
3 Tbs. powdered fruit pectin	Mint extract (optional)

Crush mint leaves and stems. Place mint and water in a 3-quart casserole. Bring to a boil, 3 to 4 minutes. Let stand 10 minutes. Strain and measure 2½ cups of liquid. Mix pectin with ¼ cup sugar. Slowly add to liquid. Add a few drops of food coloring. Cook 3 to 4 minutes. Add rest of sugar; mix well. Cook until jelly comes to a full boil, 4 to 5 minutes. Boil for 1 minute. Stir and skim. Pour into glasses or jars and seal.

Makes 2 pints.

Peach Jam
10 minutes

2 cups peach pulp
4 Tbs. powdered fruit pectin
2½ cups sugar

Peel fruit; crush thoroughly. Place in a 3-quart casserole or oval roasting dish. Stir in pectin, cover with wax paper or plastic wrap, and cook 3 minutes. Stir and cook 2 more minutes. Stir in sugar. Cook 3 minutes, stir, and cook 2 more minutes or until jam reaches a full boil. Stir and skim. Pour into glasses or jars and seal.

Makes 1½ pints.

Strawberry Jam
12 to 12½ minutes

  1 qt. strawberries
2½ Tbs. powdered
     fruit pectin
3½ cups sugar

Place washed berries in a 3-quart casserole or oval roasting dish; crush and stir in pectin. Cover with wax paper or plastic wrap. Cook 4 minutes, stir, then cook 3 to 3½ minutes or until berries begin to boil around edges of dish. Slowly stir in sugar. Cook 3 minutes, stir, then cook 2 minutes or until jam reaches a full boil. Stir and skim. Pour into glasses or jars and seal.

Makes 2½ pints.

Peach and Strawberry Jams

11
Desserts

Cakes

Thicker batters made with all-purpose flour cook best in the microwave oven. For even cooking, turn the container several times during cooking. Use foil on the corners of a square or oblong cake to prevent overbaking. Make sure foil is smooth. Always check cake at the minimum suggested time. Remember, cooking continues during cooling. If baked goods become dry around the edge, sprinkle with a little water and reheat for a few seconds.

Bake 2-layer cake mixes one layer at a time, 5 minutes each, in 8-inch pans lined with wax paper. Add or substitute fruit juices, coffee, spices, nuts, shredded coconut, or fruits for variety. For fillings, use pudding mixes or baby food strained fruits.

Baked Alaska
8 to 10 minutes

1 (9 oz.) yellow cake mix or ½ (2 layer) yellow cake mix	1 qt. raspberry sherbet
1 qt. vanilla ice cream, slightly softened	8 egg whites
	1 cup granulated sugar

Follow directions for mixing cake on package. Pour into 8-inch round cake dish lined with 2 wax-paper rounds for easy removal. Bake 4 to 5 minutes. Cool. Cut out piece of grocery-bag or other heavy brown paper at least ½ inch larger than cake layer; place on a 14 x 10-inch cookie sheet. Center cake on paper; place in freezer to chill. Line a 1½-quart mixing bowl with waxed paper or foil. Using a wooden spoon, pack vanilla ice cream along bottom and sides of dish. Fill center with raspberry sherbet. Place sheet of waxed paper on top; press top flat with palms of hands. Freeze until firm.

When ice cream is firm, make meringue by beating egg whites until they stand in moist, drooping peaks. Slowly add sugar, 2 tablespoons at a time, beating until stiff and glossy. Very quickly, invert ice cream onto cake layer. Peel off paper. Quickly cover ice cream and cake completely with meringue,

Baked Alaska

using a spatula. Return to freezer. About 15 minutes before serving, remove from freezer and brown in conventional oven, preheated to 500°, 4 to 5 minutes. Use 2 pancake turners to transfer to chilled serving plate.

Serves 8 to 12.

Fresh Apple Cake
16 to 18 minutes

1 cup sugar	1 cup sifted all-purpose flour
½ cup butter or margarine	2 tsp. baking soda
1 egg	⅛ tsp. salt
3 cups finely chopped unpeeled apples (3 medium apples)	1 tsp. cinnamon
	½ tsp. nutmeg
	½ cup finely chopped walnuts or pecans

Cream sugar and butter in large mixing bowl; beat in egg and stir in chopped apples. Sift together flour, soda, salt, cinnamon, and nutmeg. Add nuts to dry ingredients and stir into apple mixture. Spread batter in a wax-paper-lined 8-inch round cake dish. Bake 10 to 12 minutes, turning dish once. Serve with Hot Lemon Sauce.

Hot Lemon Sauce

½ cup sugar	2 Tbs. butter or margarine
1 Tbs. cornstarch	1½ Tbs. lemon juice
⅛ tsp. nutmeg	
⅛ tsp. salt	
1 cup water	

Combine sugar, cornstarch, salt, and nutmeg in a 1½-quart bowl. Heat water in measuring cup until boiling, 3 minutes. Stir boiling water gradually into sugar-cornstarch mixture until smooth. Cook 3 minutes, stirring every minute, or until slightly thickened.

Serves 8.

Golden Orange Cake
10 to 12 minutes

1 package (2 layer) yellow cake mix	1 (10 oz.) jar apricot-pineapple preserves or orange marmalade
¾ cup apricot or peach nectar	½ cup sifted confectioners sugar
1 (3 oz.) package orange flavor gelatin	
4 eggs, separated	
1 tsp. lemon extract	

Combine first 3 ingredients. Mix well. Add egg yolks, one at a time, beating after each addition. Add lemon extract. Beat egg whites stiff but not dry; fold in. Pour into two wax-paper-lined 8-inch round baking dishes. Bake, one layer at a time, 5 to 6 minutes. Spread preserves or marmalade between layers. Sift confectioners sugar over top.

Serves 16.

Busy Day Cake
6½ minutes

¼ cup butter or margarine	2½ tsp. baking powder
1¾ cups sifted all-purpose flour	½ tsp. salt
	1 unbeaten egg
	¾ cup milk
1 cup sugar	1 tsp. vanilla

Beat butter to soften. Sift dry ingredients together. Add egg and half of milk; mix until flour is dampened, then beat vigorously 2 minutes. Add remaining milk and vanilla. Beat vigorously 2 minutes longer. Pour butter into wax-paper-lined 8-inch round cake pan. Cook 6½ minutes. Frost with your favorite icing.

Serves 8.

Caramel-in-between Fudge Cake
15 to 17 minutes

28 (half 14 oz. package) light caramels	1 (17½ oz.) package fudge cake mix
1 (14 oz.) can sweetened condensed milk	1 cup water
	1 Tbs. butter or margarine
1 Tbs. butter or margarine	3 eggs

Combine caramels, sweetened condensed milk, and butter in mixing bowl. Cook until caramels are melted, 3 minutes, stirring occasionally. In large mixing bowl, combine dry cake mix, water, butter, and eggs. Beat with mixer according to package directions. Line two 8-inch round or square cake dishes with wax paper. Spread ¼ of batter in each dish. Spread half of the caramel filling evenly over batter. Cover filling with remaining batter.

Caramel-in-between Fudge Cake

Cook, one layer at a time, 6 to 7 minutes, turning dish once.

Serves 12.

Chocolate Pudding Cake
9 minutes

1 package chocolate cake mix	1 cup brown sugar
1 cup chopped nuts	⅓ cup cocoa
	½ tsp. vanilla
1½ cups boiling water	

Mix cake as directed on package. Fold in nuts. Pour into ungreased 13 x 9-inch baking dish. Combine hot water, brown sugar, cocoa, and vanilla. Pour water mixture over cake; do not stir into cake. Cook 9 minutes. Cake mixture will boil over slightly, but do not remove any batter. Let cake set 15 minutes before removing from pan.

Serves 12.

Cherry Nut Pudding Cake
16 minutes

1 (1 lb. 5 oz.) can prepared cherry pie filling	½ cup butter or margarine, melted
2 cups (half of 2 layer) yellow or white cake mix or 1 package 1-layer cake mix (9 oz.)	1 cup chopped nuts

Cherry Nut Pudding Cake

Quick Trick Fruitcake

Spread cherry pie filling in a 7 x 11-inch utility dish. Sprinkle pie filling with dry cake mix. Drizzle melted butter over mixture. Sprinkle with nuts. Bake 16 minutes, covered with paper toweling, turning dish once.

Serves 12.

Quick Trick Fruitcake
12½ to 14¼ minutes

⅔ cup water	1 tsp. cinnamon
1 (14 oz.) package date bar mix	¼ tsp. nutmeg
	¼ tsp. allspice
3 eggs	1 cup nuts, coarsely chopped
¼ cup all-purpose flour, unsifted	1 cup raisins
¾ tsp. baking powder	1 cup mixed candied fruit
2 Tbs. molasses	

Heat water until boiling in mixing bowl, 1½ to 2¼ minutes. Combine filling from date bar mix with hot water. Add crumbly mix, eggs, flour, baking powder, molasses, and spices. Mix well. Fold in nuts, raisins, and fruit. Pour into a 6-cup glass ring mold or a 2-quart casserole with a glass or small jar for tube. Cook 11 to 12 minutes, turning once. Cool 15 minutes. Remove from dish, cool completely, wrap in foil or place in container, and store in a cool place.

Serves 12.

Shortcake
5 to 6 minutes

2 cups sifted all-purpose flour	½ tsp. salt
¼ cup sugar	¼ cup butter or margarine
3 tsp. baking powder	¾ cup milk

Combine dry ingredients. Cut in butter until mixture resembles coarse crumbs. Add milk and mix until dry ingredients are moistened. Dough will be lumpy. Spread in a greased 8-inch square cake dish. Bake 4 minutes, turn dish, cook 1 to 2 more minutes. Serve with any fresh fruit, whipped cream, or ice cream.

Serves 6 to 8.

Basic Flash Frosting
9 to 12 minutes

1 cup sugar
1½ tsp. corn syrup
¼ cup hot water
2 egg whites
1 tsp. vanilla

Mix sugar, corn syrup, and water in 2-quart casserole dish. Cook until syrup spins a thread (about 240°), 9 to 12 minutes. Beat egg whites until stiff enough to hold a point. Pour hot syrup slowly into egg whites, beating constantly. Continue beating until frosting holds peaks. Blend in vanilla.

Pineapple Flash
Substitute pineapple juice for water. Fold in 2 teaspoons grated lemon rind.

Pink Party Flash
Before spreading on cake, fold in ¼ cup well-drained, finely chopped maraschino cherries.

Lemon Flash
Decrease water to 1 tablespoon; add 3 tablespoons lemon juice. After beating, fold in 1 teaspoon lemon rind and ½ teaspoon almond extract.

Seafoam Flash
Substitute 1 cup brown sugar, firmly packed, for 1 cup granulated sugar.

Chocolate Flash
Fold in 1 square (1 ounce) unsweetened chocolate, coarsely ground, after beating.

Marshmallow Flash
Fold in 6 to 8 quartered marshmallows after beating.

Makes enough to frost 2 8-inch layers.

Fruit

Cooked by microwave, fruits have a better taste, color, and texture then when cooked conventionally. The amount of sugar varies with the fruit used, so cooking times will differ.

Apple Crisp
12 to 14 minutes

6 medium cooking apples, peeled and sliced	½ cup packed brown sugar
¼ cup granulated sugar	¾ cup sifted flour
½ tsp. cinnamon	½ tsp. salt
¼ tsp. cloves	½ cup butter or margarine
2 tsp. lemon juice	¼ cup chopped nuts

Pare, core, and slice apples. Combine sugar, cinnamon, cloves, and lemon juice and mix with fruit; place in 8 x 8-inch glass baking dish.

Apple Crisp

Crumble together brown sugar, flour, salt, and butter. Mix in nuts and sprinkle over apples. Cook, uncovered, 12 to 14 minutes or until apples are tender.

Serves 6 to 8.

Cinnamon Apples
5 minutes

- 4 medium baking apples
- 4 tsp. cinnamon candies

Wash and core apples. Place in 1½-quart casserole. Fill center of apples with candies. Cover with paper toweling. Cook 5 minutes. Spoon juice over apples.

Serves 4.

Cinnamon Apples

Brazilian Bananas

Brazilian Bananas

3½ to 5¾ minutes

¼ cup butter or margarine	⅛ tsp. cinnamon
6 ripe, firm bananas, peeled	⅛ tsp. allspice
1 Tbs. lemon juice	⅔ cup shredded coconut
¼ cup packed brown sugar	

Melt butter in 7 x 11-inch baking dish, 30 to 45 seconds. Roll bananas in butter to coat well. Sprinkle with lemon juice. Combine brown sugar, cinnamon, and allspice; sprinkle over bananas. Bake 2 to 3 minutes. Sprinkle with coconut; cook 1 to 2 minutes longer or until soft.

Serves 6.

Blueberry Peach Compote

1 to 1½ minutes

⅓ cup water	3 cups (about 8 medium) sliced fresh ripe peaches
¾ cup sugar	
Dash of salt	
2 cinnamon sticks	
1 tsp. fresh lemon juice	1 cup fresh blueberries
	Fresh mint

Combine water, sugar, salt, and cinnamon sticks in 2-quart casserole. Mix well and cook until boiling, 1 to 1½ minutes. Add lemon juice; stir. Cool slightly. Remove cinnamon sticks and stir in mixed fruit. Garnish with mint. Serve warm or chilled.

Serves 6.

Cherries Jubilee

7¾ to 9¾ minutes

2 (10 oz.) packages frozen Bing cherries	2 Tbs. rum or brandy
2 tsp. sugar	Vanilla ice cream
2 tsp. cornstarch	

Thaw cherries in box on paper towel, 3 to 3½ minutes. Place a colander in a 1-quart casserole dish. Drain thawed cherries. Combine sugar and cornstarch with cherry juice. Cook until slightly thick and clear, 3 to 4 minutes, stirring after each minute. Add drained cherries and heat 1½ to 2 minutes.

Heat rum or brandy in custard or measuring cup for 10 to 15 seconds. Add to cherry mixture, ignite, and spoon carefully over ice cream.

Serves 4 to 6.

Peaches in Wine

6½ to 7¾ minutes

3 Tbs. butter	⅓ cup brown sugar
2 Tbs. lemon juice	⅓ cup rosé wine
1 can (1 lb. 13 oz.) peach halves or slices, drained	½ cup heavy cream

Melt butter in 2 quart casserole, 30 to 45 seconds. Add lemon juice and peaches. Turn peaches over to coat with butter. Sprinkle with brown sugar and add wine. Cook 3 minutes. Stir in cream. Cover and cook 3 to 4 minutes. Serve warm.

Serves 6.

Peaches in Wine

Baked Stuffed Pears

Spicy Fruit Compote

Baked Stuffed Pears
6 to 7 minutes

3 large ripe fresh
   pears, halved,
   pared, and cored
½ cup orange or
   kumquat
   marmalade
½ cup chopped nuts

Place pear halves, cut side up, in an 8-inch round baking dish. Fill each half with marmalade; sprinkle with nuts. Cover with plastic wrap and cook 4 minutes. Turn dish, cook 2 to 3 minutes longer. Serve warm or cold.
   Serves 6.

Spicy Fruit Compote
6 to 7 minutes

1 (1 lb.) can fruit
   for salads
1 (13 oz.) can
   pineapple
   chunks
1 tart apple,
   unpeeled, cored,
   and cubed
1 Tbs. lemon juice
¼ tsp. ground
   nutmeg

¼ tsp. ground
   cinnamon
⅛ tsp. ground
   cloves
⅓ cup brown sugar
¼ cup butter or
   margarine
1 cup fresh
   seedless grapes
2 bananas, peeled
   and sliced

Drain syrup from canned fruit. Place canned fruit and apple in a 2½-quart casserole. Add lemon juice, spices, and sugar. Dot with butter; cover and cook 4 to 5 minutes. Add grapes and bananas; cover and cook 2 minutes. Serve hot.
   Serves 12.

Pies

Piecrusts made with cracker or cookie crumbs can be baked in the microwave oven. Pastry shells can be made in ovens with a browning unit. Those that do best use milk, instead of water, and a yellow shortening. Do not prick pastry crust as the prick marks bake shut when cooked by microwave.

For pie filling, use canned fruits or berries with a crumble topping, or pudding mixes cooked in the oven. For variety, add swirled chocolate, shredded coconut, slivered almonds, or sliced bananas to vanilla mixes.

Pastry Shell
6 to 6½ minutes, in browning-unit oven only

½ cup all-purpose
   flour
½ tsp. salt
6 Tbs. yellow
   vegetable
   shortening
3 Tbs. milk

Mix together flour and salt. Cut in shortening and sprinkle with milk. Gather dough together and roll out ⅛-inch-thick pastry shell. Put shell into 9-inch pie plate, making certain pastry is not stretched and fits well into plate. Build up edge above edge of plate and flute. Do not make edge too thick. Do not prick shell. Cover shell completely with a paper towel and

fit a second pie plate (8-inch) inside to prevent shrinkage and bubbling of crust. Cook 3½ minutes. Remove top plate and paper towel, being careful not to tear shell. Cook 2½ to 3 minutes longer, browning simultaneously or after cooking is completed. Cool.
Makes 1 9-inch crust.

Graham Cracker Crust
1½ to 2 minutes

1½ cups graham cracker crumbs (18 to 20 crackers)	⅓ cup butter or margarine, melted
	¼ cup sugar

Combine all ingredients. Mix well. Press evenly into a 9-inch pie plate. Bake 1½ to 2 minutes. Cool before filling.

You may use gingersnaps or chocolate or vanilla wafers instead of graham crackers, and omit the sugar.
Makes 1 9-inch crust.

Butterscotch Peach Pie
7½ to 9 minutes

2 (1 lb. 13 oz.) cans sliced peaches	¼ cup peach syrup
1 baked pie shell	¼ cup butter or margarine
½ cup brown sugar	2 tsp. lemon juice
2 Tbs. flour	
⅛ tsp. salt	

Butterscotch Peach Pie

Drain peaches and reserve syrup. Place peaches in baked pie shell. In a mixing bowl combine sugar, flour, salt, and peach syrup. Stir well, add butter, and cook until thick, 1½ to 2 minutes, stirring once. Add lemon juice. Pour over peaches and cook 6 to 7 minutes. Pie will set more as it cools.
Serves 8.

Honey Pecan Pie
3¾ to 6¼ minutes

1 (9 in.) baked pie shell	¼ cup butter or margarine
Flour	3 eggs, beaten
½ cup honey	1 cup chopped pecans
½ cup light brown sugar, packed	

Dust pie shell well with flour. Pour honey and sugar into a 1-quart casserole dish. Heat to form a smooth syrup, ¾ to 1¼ minutes. Add butter, beaten eggs, and nuts. Pour into pie shell. Cook 3 to 5 minutes. Center of pie will be soft, but becomes firm when cool.
Serves 8.

Apricot Crumble Pie
8 to 12 minutes

1 (9 in.) baked pastry shell	½ tsp. cinnamon
1 cup sugar	⅓ cup butter or margarine
4 cups fresh apricots, cut up	⅔ cup sifted all-purpose flour
4 Tbs. lemon juice	½ cup sugar
4 Tbs. cornstarch	
½ tsp. nutmeg	

Sprinkle pastry shell with one tablespoon flour, covering bottom and sides. Combine sugar, apricots, lemon juice, cornstarch, and spices in 1½-quart bowl. In another small bowl, cut butter into flour and sugar; set aside for crumble topping. Cook apricot mixture 6 to 8 minutes, stirring after every 2 minutes. Pour into baked shell and sprinkle with topping. Cook 2 to 3 minutes using browning unit or under conventional broiler 2 to 4 minutes until topping is brown and bubbly.
Serves 8.

Fresh Strawberry Glaze Pie
4 to 5 minutes

1 (9 in.) graham
  cracker
  piecrust
Powdered sugar
2 cups
  strawberries,
  mashed
1¼ cups sugar
3 Tbs. cornstarch

1 Tbs. lemon
  juice
Few drops of red
  food coloring
  (optional)
2 cups whole
  strawberries,
  drained well

Make piecrust. Sprinkle with powdered sugar. Place mashed berries in a 1½-quart casserole dish. Mix the sugar and cornstarch together; add to mashed berries. Cook until thick and clear, 4 to 5 minutes, stirring after one minute, then every 30 seconds. Remove from oven and add lemon juice; stir. Allow to cool. Place 1 cup of the whole berries in piecrust. Spoon ⅓ of glaze over the berries. Add remaining whole berries and pour remaining glaze evenly over entire pie. Chill for 3 to 4 hours. Serve with whipped cream as desired.

Serves 8.

Walnut Pie
12 to 13 minutes

1 cup honey
1 package (3¼ oz.)
  vanilla instant
  pudding
¾ cup undiluted
  evaporated milk
¼ tsp. salt

2 eggs, slightly
  beaten
1 cup coarsely
  broken walnuts
1 (9 in.) graham
  cracker pie shell

In mixing bowl, blend honey with instant pudding. Gradually add milk, salt, and eggs. Mix until well blended. Fold in walnuts. Cook, uncovered, 4 minutes, stirring twice. Pour into baked pie shell. Cook 8 to 9 minutes. Refrigerate. Serve cold. Remove from refrigerator 20 minutes before serving.

Serves 8.

Puddings

Puddings continue to cook after removal from the oven. Overcooking will cause them to separate and become too thin. The center will not be completely set until it has cooled. Allow all desserts to stand 5 minutes before serving.

Walnut Pie

Eggnog Pudding

Bread 'n' Butter Pudding

6½ to 9 minutes

2 cups soft bread cubes with crusts	½ cup sugar
	⅓ cup raisins, chopped nuts, or dates
¼ cup butter or margarine, melted	1 tsp. vanilla
⅔ cup milk	Vanilla ice cream (optional)
3 eggs	

Measure bread into a greased 1½-quart casserole. Melt butter in a 4-cup measuring cup or bowl, 30 seconds to 1 minute. Pour over bread; toss. In same measuring cup, measure milk, add eggs, beat until foamy. Stir in sugar, raisins, and vanilla. Pour over bread cubes, mixing well. Cook 6 to 8 minutes, stirring after 3 or 4 minutes. Serve warm, with or without ice cream.

Serves 6.

Eggnog Pudding

6 to 6½ minutes

1 package (3¼ oz.) vanilla pudding mix	¼ tsp. nutmeg
	½ cup heavy cream, whipped
1 cup milk	Maraschino cherries
1 cup dairy eggnog	

Place pudding in a 1½-quart casserole dish. Add milk gradually, stirring to dissolve pudding; stir in eggnog and cook until pudding thickens, 3 minutes. Stir, cook 3 to 3½ minutes longer, stirring occasionally. Add nutmeg and cool. Spoon into dishes and decorate with whipped cream and maraschino cherries.

Serves 6.

Pumpkin Pudding

14 to 18 minutes

1⅔ cups sifted all-purpose flour	½ cup shortening
	1 cup pumpkin, cooked or canned
1⅓ cups sugar	⅓ cup water
1 tsp. soda	1 egg
½ tsp. salt	1 cup chopped dates
¼ tsp. baking powder	½ cup chopped nuts
½ tsp. cinnamon	
¼ tsp. cloves	

Sift flour, sugar, soda, salt, baking powder, and spices together into a mixing bowl. Add shortening, pumpkin and water. Beat 2 minutes at a medium speed with electric mixer. Scrape sides and bottom of bowl. Add egg and dates. Beat 2 minutes longer. Mix in nuts. Pour evenly into two greased 8-inch round dishes. Cook 7 to 9 minutes for each dish, turning after 5 minutes. Serve warm with sauce.

Creamy Sauce

1 egg	1 cup whipping cream
1 Tbs. melted butter or margarine	½ tsp. vanilla
1¼ cups confectioner's sugar	

Beat egg until foamy. Stir in melted butter. Add sugar and beat until smooth. Whip cream until stiff. Blend whipped cream and vanilla with egg and sugar mixture.

Serves 12.

Low-Fat Rice Pudding

Low-Fat Rice Pudding

11 to 14 minutes

2 packages (2¼ oz.) imitation custard dessert mix
4 cups nonfat milk
4 cups cooked rice, room temperature
1½ cups raisins
Nutmeg

In a 2-quart casserole, mix custard as directed on box, using nonfat milk. Stir to dissolve mix. Add cooked rice and raisins. Stir. Pour into 7 x 11-inch utility dish. Sprinkle with nutmeg. Cook 11 to 14 minutes, stirring after every 3 minutes.

Serves 6 to 8.

Toppings

Hot Fudge Sauce

1¾ to 3 minutes

1 can (15 oz.) sweetened condensed milk
¼ cup butter or margarine
Dash of salt
1 package (6 oz.) chocolate chips
½ tsp. vanilla
5 Tbs. strong coffee
½ cup chopped nuts (optional)

Combine milk, butter, and salt in a 1-quart bowl or measuring cup. Bring to a boil, 1½ to 2½ minutes, stirring every minute. Add chocolate chips, stirring until melted, heating an additional 15 to 30 seconds if necessary. Blend in vanilla and coffee; fold in nuts. Serve warm over ice cream. May be reheated, 15 to 45 seconds.

Makes 2¼ cups.

Dessert Lemon Sauce

2 minutes

½ cup sugar
1 Tbs. cornstarch
1 cup water
2 Tbs. butter or margarine
½ tsp. grated lemon peel
1½ Tbs. lemon juice
Dash of salt

In a 1-quart glass casserole, combine sugar and cornstarch. Stir in water and heat, uncovered, 2 minutes, stirring every 30 seconds. Add butter, lemon peel, lemon juice, and salt. Mix well. Serve warm or cold over pound cake, sponge cake, angel food cake, or gingerbread.

Serves 6 to 8.

Fudge Marshmallow Topping

4 minutes

1 cup packed brown sugar
¼ cup cocoa
½ cup milk
1 Tbs. butter or margarine
1 tsp. vanilla
1 cup miniature marshmallows
½ cup chopped walnuts or pecans (optional)

Mix brown sugar and cocoa together in 1½-quart casserole. Stir in milk. Cook 4 minutes, stirring frequently. Add butter and vanilla. Cool 5 minutes; fold in marshmallows. Serve warm over vanilla ice cream. Top with nuts if desired.

Makes 1¼ cups.

Hot Fudge Sauce

Butterscotch Brownies

12
Cookies and Confections

Cookies

Bar cookies do extremely well in the microwave oven. Use one or more 8-inch square or 7 x 10-inch baking pans. Covering the corners of the pan smoothly with foil helps to prevent overbaking. Turn the container during cooking time. Using a paper towel over the dish helps to prevent cookies from becoming hard and dry. All cookies should stand 5 minutes before serving. They may be placed under the conventional broiler for about 2 minutes for a browner appearance.

Butterscotch Brownies
5 minutes

¼ cup butter or margarine, melted
1 cup brown sugar.
1 egg, beaten
1 tsp. vanilla
½ cup flour
1 tsp. baking powder
½ tsp. salt
½ cup nuts, chopped

Melt butter in mixing bowl. Stir in brown sugar. Allow to cool slightly. Add egg and vanilla, mix well. Sift dry ingredients together. Stir into butter mixture. Add nuts and spread evenly in an 8-inch square baking dish lined with wax paper. Bake 5 minutes. Cool. Cut into bars.
Makes 16.

Chewy Mint Squares
5 to 6 minutes

½ cup butter or margarine
¼ cup plus 2 Tbs. white sugar
¼ cup plus 2 Tbs. packed brown sugar
½ tsp. vanilla
1 egg
1 cup sifted all-purpose flour
½ tsp. baking soda
½ tsp. salt
½ cup coarsely chopped walnuts
6 chocolate-covered mints, cut into small pieces

Cream butter, sugars, and vanilla thoroughly. Beat in egg. Blend in flour, soda, and salt. Mix in walnuts. Spread in well-greased 7 x 11-inch utility dish. Sprinkle mint pieces over top of batter. Bake 5 to 6 minutes. Cool. Cut into squares.

Makes 24.

Chocolate Chip Meringue Bars
9½ to 10 minutes

½ cup butter or margarine, melted	½ cup boiling water
1 package fudge cake mix	½ cup chopped pecans or walnuts
2 eggs, beaten	½ cup semisweet chocolate bits
1 package fluffy white frosting mix	

Melt butter in oven, ½ to 1 minute. In large mixing bowl, combine with cake mix and eggs. Stir by hand until well combined. Press in ungreased 7 x 11-inch utility dish. Prepare frosting with boiling water as directed on package. Spread on batter; keep frosting about 2 inches from dish edge; frosting will spread while baking. Sprinkle nuts and chocolate pieces over frosting. Bake 9 minutes, turning dish once. Cool. Cut into bars.

Makes 24.

Chocolate Chip Meringue Bars

Fudgie Peanut Butter Bars
12 to 15 minutes

½ cup butter or margarine	1 (14 oz.) can sweetened, condensed milk
1 package (2 layer) yellow cake mix	2 Tbs. butter or margarine
1 cup peanut butter	1 package coconut pecan frosting mix
2 eggs	
1 cup semisweet chocolate pieces	

Melt butter in oven, ½ to 1 minute. Combine in large bowl with cake mix, peanut butter, butter, and eggs. Stir dough until it holds together. Press two-thirds of dough into bottom of ungreased 7 x 11-inch utility dish. Reserve remaining dough for topping. Prepare filling by combining chocolate pieces, sweetened condensed milk, and butter in 2-quart mixing bowl. Cook until chocolate is melted and mixture is smooth, 1½ to 2 minutes. Stir in frosting mix. Spread filling over dough in dish. Crumble reserved dough over filling. Bake 10 to 12 minutes. Warm before serving.

Makes 24.

Fudgie Peanut Butter Bars

Graham Cracker Pralines

Graham Cracker Pralines

6 to 7½ minutes

1 cup butter	60 graham
1 cup firmly	crackers (1 x 2
packed brown	in. size)
sugar	
1 cup chopped	
pecans	

Cream butter and sugar; add nuts. Spread 1 heaping teaspoonful evenly on each cracker. Cook in 7 x 11 inch utility dish, 20 crackers at a time, 2 to 2½ minutes. Let stand 3 to 4 minutes. Remove from dish and place on paper plates or towels. Let stand 5 to 10 minutes to cool and crisp. Watch pralines while cooking. The butter will burn quickly. Pralines do not have to brown to become crisp.

Makes 60.

Mexican Chocolate Bars

7 to 8¾ minutes

½ cup butter or	2 squares
margarine	unsweetened
2 eggs	chocolate
1 cup sugar	1 cup walnuts,
½ cup flour	chopped
¼ tsp. salt	½ tsp. vanilla
½ tsp. cinnamon	Powdered sugar
¼ tsp. cloves	

Melt butter in mixing bowl, 30 to 45 seconds. Add eggs and sugar and beat well. Add flour, salt, cinnamon, and cloves. Stir well. Melt chocolate in 1-cup measurer, 1½ to 2 minutes. Add melted chocolate, nuts, and vanilla to mix. Spread in unlined 1½-quart (10 x 6-inch) baking dish. Cook 5 to 6 minutes. Cut while warm; sprinkle with powdered sugar.

Makes 24.

Confections

Be sure to cook candy in a large bowl to prevent boilovers, especially if the recipe calls for milk. Watch closely during cooking and be patient about cooling. If using a candy thermometer, *do not* put the thermometer in the oven when it is on.

Butterscotch Crunchies

2 to 2½ minutes

2 (6 oz.) packages	6 cups cornflakes
butterscotch	or similar flakes
pieces	
½ cup peanut	
butter	

Place butterscotch pieces and peanut butter in a large mixing bowl. Cook until mixture melts, 2 to 2½ minutes. Stir in flakes; mix well. Drop by teaspoonful onto wax paper. Let set.

Makes 36.

Butterscotch Crunchies

Chocolate Noodle Candy

1 to 2 minutes

  1 (6 oz.) package
    chocolate chips
  1 (5 oz.) can chow
    mein noodles
  1 cup chopped nuts

In large mixing bowl, melt chocolate, 1 to 2 minutes. Stir. Add noodles and nuts. Mix well. Drop by teaspoons onto wax-paper-covered cookie sheet. Refrigerate until firm, 15 to 30 minutes.

Chocolate will continue to melt after removal from oven. Watch carefully so it does not boil.

Makes 24.

Nutted Candycorn

6 to 10 minutes

  2 cups sugar   2 Tbs. vinegar
  1 cup molasses   ½ tsp. soda
  1 Tbs. butter or   1 cup peanuts
    margarine   4 cups popped corn

Combine sugar, molasses, butter, and vinegar in a 1½-quart mixing bowl. Cook until mixture reaches the hard crack stage (300°), 6 to 10 minutes, stirring every minute. Add soda and stir briskly. Combine peanuts and corn in large bowl. Pour hot sugar mixture over them. Stir until well coated.

Makes 5 cups.

Chocolate Noodle Candy

Frosting Mix Fudge

Frosting Mix Fudge

2¾ to 3¼ minutes

  3 Tbs. butter or
    margarine
  3 Tbs. water
  1 (13 to 15 oz.)
    package
    chocolate fudge
    frosting mix

Melt butter in water in a 2-quart casserole dish, 30 to 45 seconds. Add frosting mix; stir well. Cook 1¼ to 1½ minutes or until mixture comes to a full boil. Boil for 1 minute. Pour into 8 or 9-inch square pan or utility dish. Cut into squares while still warm.

Before pouring into buttered dish, you may add ½ to 1 cup chopped nuts, ¼ cup finely cut up candied cherries, ½ cup seedless raisins, or ½ cup flaked coconut, toasted if you prefer. Other frosting mixes can also be used; milk can be used in place of water.

Makes 1 pound.

Caramel Apples

3 to 4 minutes

 49 (14 oz. bag)
    caramels
  2 Tbs. water
  4 to 5 medium
    apples
Wooden sticks

Melt caramels with water in 1-quart casserole dish 3 to 4 minutes, stirring after 1 minute, then every 30 seconds. Stir with wooden spoon which can be left in dish while cooking. Wash and dry apples and insert a wooden stick into stem end of each. Dip apples in hot caramel sauce; turn until well coated. Scrape off excess sauce from bottom of apples. Place on greased wax paper; chill until firm. Keep in cool place.

Makes 4 to 5.

Halloween Popcorn Balls
6½ to 12½ minutes

7 cups popped corn	1 tsp. vanilla
1 cup sugar	Few drops red and
⅓ cup water	yellow food
⅓ cup light corn	coloring
syrup	Gumdrops and
1 tsp. salt	candy corn
¼ cup butter or	
margarine	

Put popped corn in bowl. Mix sugar, water, syrup, salt, and butter in 2-quart casserole dish. Cook 1½ minutes, stir, cook 5 to 11 minutes longer or until syrup reaches 250°, or hard-boil stage. Remove from heat. Stir in vanilla. Add food coloring to make color syrup

orange. Pour in thin stream over corn, stirring constantly to mix well. With buttered hands, form into pumpkin shapes. Use small gumdrops for eyes and nose, candy corn for teeth, green gumdrops for stem.

Makes 12 to 15.

Nuts and Bolts
6 to 8 minutes

¾ cup butter or margarine	1 (6¾ oz.) can cocktail peanuts
3 Tbs. Worcestershire sauce	1 (6 oz.) can mixed nuts or cashews
2 tsp. garlic salt	2 cups Wheat Chex
2 tsp. onion salt	2 cups Rice Chex
2 tsp. celery salt	2 cups Cheerios
1 (10 oz.) box thin pretzels	

Melt butter in 3-quart bowl, 30 seconds to 1 minute. Add Worcestershire sauce and salts and mix well. Stir in the remaining ingredients and toss until well coated. Cook 6 to 8 minutes, stirring every 2 minutes. Cool and store in a tightly covered container.

Makes 10 cups.

Halloween Popcorn Balls

Seasoned Pecans and Nuts and Bolts

Seasoned Pecans

4½ to 4¾ minutes

- 2 cups pecan halves
- 2 Tbs. butter or margarine
- 1 Tbs. seasoned salt

Melt butter in round or square baking dish, 30 to 45 seconds. Stir in seasoned salt; add nuts and mix well to coat nuts with seasoned butter. Cook 4 minutes, stirring twice. Serve warm or cold.

Makes 2 cups.

Salted Garlic Almonds

14½ to 17 minutes

- 1 lb. almonds
- ¼ cup salad oil or olive oil
- Salt
- 1 clove garlic

Blanch almonds by putting 2 cups water in 2-quart casserole. When it reaches boiling point, drop almonds into water. Cover, cook 3½ to 4 minutes. Let stand 5 minutes. Drain and remove skins. Dry almonds. Put salad oil in 2-quart utility dish. Crush garlic and add to oil. Heat 3 to 4 minutes. Discard garlic. Add almonds and stir well to coat with oil. Cook 8 to 9 minutes, stirring every 2 or 3 minutes. If you have a browning unit, use for 5 minutes. Drain on paper towels, sprinkle with salt to taste. ready to eat. Almonds should be lightly browned.

Makes 3 cups.

Toffee Almonds

2½ to 3 minutes

- 1 cup whole blanched almonds
- ½ cup sugar
- 2 Tbs. butter
- ½ tsp. vanilla

Mix almonds, sugar, and butter in 1-quart casserole dish or 1-quart glass measuring cup. Heat 1 minute, stir, cook 1½ to 2 minutes longer, until sugar is a light golden brown. Add vanilla. Spread nuts on a piece of foil; sprinkle with salt. Cool. Break into small pieces.

Makes 1 cup.

Toffee Almonds and Salted Garlic Almonds

13
Breads

Muffins can be cooked in glass custard cups with paper cupcake liners. If you do not have custard cups, use two or three thicknesses of paper liners. Sprinkle sweet muffins with a sugar and cinnamon mixture to give a browned appearance.

Try using your own recipe for coffee cakes and quick breads. Should your recipe have more batter than one dish will hold (filling about half full) bake in two layers. One layer can be frozen for later use. Or you can divide your recipe in half. Be sure not to overcook quick breads.

Cover corners of square or oblong baking dishes with foil to prevent overbaking. Be sure foil is smooth. Place a paper towel over a dish of batter to obtain even baking.

Breads and rolls can be heated in serving plate or basket. Always put paper toweling, or cloth or paper under bread items before heating. Rolls can be heated in a paper bag, but do not close end of bag tightly. Heat only until outside is warm to the touch.

Heating Chart for Bread Items

	Room Temperature	Frozen
Sweet or dinner rolls—1 item	15 seconds	20 seconds
Each additional item, add	5 seconds	10 seconds
Bread slices—1 item	10 seconds	15 seconds
Each additional item, add	5 seconds	10 seconds
Doughnuts—1 item	10 seconds	25 seconds
Each additional items, add	5 seconds	10 seconds
Bagels—English muffins—1 item	10 seconds	20 seconds
Each additional item, add	5 seconds	10 seconds
Coffee cake or loaf	1 to 1½ minutes	1½ to 2 minutes

Heating Chart for Bread Items

	Refrigerated	Frozen
Pancakes—1 item	20 seconds	45 seconds
Each additional item add	15 seconds	25 seconds
Waffles—1 item	15 seconds	20 seconds
Each additional item add	10 seconds	15 seconds
French toast—1 item	30 seconds	1 minute
Each additional item add	15 seconds	1 minute

Banana Nut Bread

Sticky Biscuit Wreath

Banana Nut Bread
9½ to 10½ minutes

¼ cup butter or margarine	1½ cups all-purpose flour
½ cup sugar	½ tsp. salt
1 egg, well beaten	1 tsp. baking powder
1 cup bran	½ tsp. soda
1½ cup mashed bananas	1 tsp. vanilla
2 Tbs. water	½ cup chopped nuts

Cream butter and sugar; add egg, then bran; mix thoroughly. Combine bananas and water. Sift together flour, salt, baking powder, and soda. Add alternately with bananas. Mix well; add vanilla and nuts. Pour into 9 x 5-inch loaf dish. Cook 9½ to 10½ minutes. Cool 15 minutes. Remove from dish. Serve warm or cold. Serves 8.

Sticky Biscuit Wreath
3½ to 4 minutes

2 Tbs. butter or margarine	⅓ cup white sugar
2 Tbs. brown sugar	1 tsp. cinnamon
¼ cup sliced almonds	1 package (8 oz.) refrigerated biscuits
6 candied or maraschino cherries cut in half	

In a 6-inch glass tube dish or 1½-quart casserole with a custard cup in center, melt butter and brown sugar 1 minute. Stir. Place almonds and cherries, cut side up, on sugar mixture. Combine white sugar and cinnamon in a small bowl. Cut each biscuit into quarters; roll in sugar-cinnamon mixture. Place in layers in dish on top of cherries and almonds. Cook, uncovered, 2½ to 3 minutes. Let stand 2 minutes. Remove custard cup, if used. Invert onto serving dish. Serve warm.

Serves 4.

Blueberry Muffins
5 to 6 minutes

1¾ cups all-purpose flour	⅓ cup salad oil or melted shortening
2 Tbs. sugar	1 (16 oz.) can blueberries, drained
2¼ tsp. baking powder	2 Tbs. sugar
1 beaten egg	
½ cup milk	

Sift dry ingredients into mixing bowl; make well in center. Combine egg, milk, and salad oil. Add all at once to dry ingredients. Stir quickly, only until dry ingredients are moistened. Combine blueberries and sugar, toss lightly. Stir gently into batter. Fill paper-lined custard cups ⅔ full. Arrange 6 custard cups in a circle and bake 2½ to 3 minutes. Repeat for second 6 cups.

Makes 12.

Bran Buttermilk Muffins
6 to 6½ minutes

½ cup sugar	½ tsp. baking soda
⅓ cup shortening	½ tsp. salt
1 egg	2 cups raisin bran flakes
1 cup sifted all-purpose flour	1 cup buttermilk
2 tsp. baking powder	

Cream together sugar, shortening, and egg until light and fluffy. Sift together flour, baking powder, soda, and salt; stir in bran flakes. Add dry ingredients to creamed mixture alternately with buttermilk. Stir just until combined. Fill paper-lined custard cups ⅔ full. Arrange 6 custard cups in a circle and bake 3 to 3¼ minutes. Repeat for second 6 cups.

Makes 12.

Buttermilk Cornbread
4½ to 5¼ minutes

1 cup self-rising flour	¾ cup buttermilk
1 cup yellow cornmeal	½ cup milk
½ tsp. baking soda	¼ cup salad oil or melted bacon drippings
2 to 4 Tbs. sugar	Bacon bits (optional)
1 egg	

Blueberry Muffins

Mix dry ingredients in a mixing bowl. Make a well in the center. Beat egg, buttermilk, milk, and oil together; pour into well in dry ingredients. Add bacon bits. Mix together just until dry ingredients are thoroughly moistened. Pour batter into a lightly greased 8-inch round or square baking dish. Bake 4½ to 5¼ minutes, turning dish once.

If you prefer all-purpose flour, use 1 cup sifted flour, 1½ teaspoons baking powder, ½ teaspoon salt, and ½ teaspoon baking soda.

Milk cartons make excellent containers for cooking this recipe. Soak 4 ½-gallon cartons in cold water, wash well, and cut down to a depth of 4½ inches. Grease insides lightly. Place a square of baking parchment or wax paper in the bottom of each container. Divide batter evenly among the 4 containers and shake down. Group containers as closely together as possible and mark inner corners. Bake 2 to 2½ minutes. Regroup cartons so marks are on outside corners. Cook 2½ to 2¾ minutes longer.

Serves 6.

Cranberry Nut Bread
8½ to 9½ minutes

2½ cups biscuit mix	¾ cups chopped
½ cup sugar	cranberries
¼ cup flour	½ cup chopped
1 egg	nuts
1 cup milk	
2 Tbs. grated	
orange peel	

Cranberry Nut Bread

Combine mix, sugar, flour, egg, milk, and orange peel and beat vigorously. Chop cranberries in blender and add to mix. Stir in nuts. Pour batter into 9 x 5-inch loaf pan. Cook 8½ to 9½ minutes or until toothpick inserted in center comes out clean. Cool before slicing.

Serves 8.

Roquefort Muffins
20 to 25 seconds

½ cup butter or	½ tsp. paprika
margarine	Pinch of onion salt
4 oz. Roquefort	4 English muffins,
cheese	sliced in half
1 tsp. salt	

Cream butter, cheese, salt, paprika, and onion salt together in a small bowl. Spread on toasted muffins. Place muffins in 7 x 11-inch baking dish. Heat 20 to 25 seconds.

Serves 4 to 6.

Zucchini Bread
9½ to 11 minutes

1 egg, beaten	1½ cups flour
1 cup cooking oil	½ tsp. baking
1 cup sugar	soda
1 tsp. vanilla	¼ tsp. baking
1 cup ground raw	powder
zucchini,	½ tsp. salt
unpared	1 tsp. cinnamon
½ cup chopped	
walnuts	

Zucchini Bread

Combine egg, oil, sugar, and vanilla. Stir well; add ground raw zucchini and walnuts. Combine flour, soda, baking powder, salt, and cinnamon. Add to zucchini mixture. Pour into a 2-quart 9 x 5-inch loaf dish. Cook 9½ to 11 minutes.

Serves 8.

Hungarian Coffee Cake
6 to 7 minutes

½ cup butter or margarine	1 Tbs. lemon rind
¾ cup sugar	2 Tbs. lemon juice
2 eggs	½ cup chopped pecans
1 cup sifted flour	2 Tbs. sugar
1 tsp. baking powder	¼ tsp. cinnamon
½ tsp. salt	

Cream butter and sugar. Add eggs one at a time, mixing thoroughly. Sift together flour, baking powder, and salt. Gradually stir in dry ingredients. Add lemon rind and juice and pecans. Turn into wax-paper-lined 8-inch round baking dish. Combine sugar and cinnamon. Sprinkle over batter. Cover with paper toweling. Cook 6 to 7 minutes, or until toothpick inserted near center comes out clean.

Serves 6.

Streusel-filled Coffee Cake
5½ to 6 minutes

1½ cups unsifted all-purpose flour	2 Tbs. melted butter or margarine
1½ tsp. baking powder	½ cup firmly packed brown sugar
¼ tsp. salt	2 tsp. cinnamon
¾ cup sugar	½ cup chopped nuts
¼ cup cooking oil	
1 egg	
½ cup milk	

In mixing bowl, combine flour, baking powder, salt, sugar, oil, egg, and milk. Mix until smooth. In smaller bowl, combine the melted butter, brown sugar, cinnamon, and nuts. Pour half of the flour mixture into a 2-quart (7 x 11-inch) baking dish. Top with half of the filling. Pour remaining flour mixture on top of filling; pour remaining filling on top. Cover with paper toweling and cook 5½ to 6 minutes or until a toothpick inserted in center comes out clean. Cake will still look moist on top.

Serves 8.

Hot Tomato Toddy

14
Beverages

Toddies and other hot beverages can be prepared almost instantly in a microwave oven. Use mugs or china cups that do not have a metal trim; for several servings, use a glass pitcher that is oven safe. Starting with hot tap water will cut cooking time even further. Heat beverages uncovered, and stir before serving to distribute heat. Add approximately 1 minute for each additional cup, as follows:

1 cup	2 cups	3 cups	4 cups
1 to 1½ minutes	2 to 2½ minutes	3 to 4 minutes	4 to 5 minutes

Hot Tomato Toddy
6 to 8 minutes

  1 can tomato soup
  1 can beef broth
  1 soup can water
  ¼ tsp. thyme
  ¼ tsp. marjoram
  ¼ tsp. oregano
  Celery salt
  Butter or margarine

Combine all ingredients except celery salt and butter. Pour into four 8-ounce china or pottery mugs. Heat 6 to 8 minutes. Sprinkle each mug with celery salt and dot with butter, then serve.

Makes 4 servings.

Cinnamon Apple Punch

Cinnamon Apple Punch
12 to 15 minutes

2 qts. apple juice	½ tsp. ground
½ cup orange juice	cloves
⅓ cup red hot	1 jar apple slices,
candies	drained

Combine all ingredients except apple slices in a 3-quart bowl. Heat thoroughly, 12 to 15 minutes, stirring occasionally. Pour into punch bowl and garnish with apple slices. Or heat individual servings in mugs or cups and garnish with apple slices.

Serves 10.

Warming Winter Punch
12 to 15 minutes

½ cup granulated sugar	4 cups freshly squeezed orange juice
½ cup firmly packed brown sugar	2 cups pineapple juice
2 cups water	½ cup freshly squeezed lemon juice
4 sticks cinnamon	1 orange, unpeeled
¼ tsp. whole cloves	1 lemon, unpeeled

In a 3-quart casserole, combine sugars, water, and spices. Bring to a boil: 5 to 6 minutes. Stir. Add orange, pineapple, and lemon juices, and heat but do not boil: 7 to 9 minutes.

Slice unpeeled fruit into cartwheels, discarding end cuts. Slice cartwheels in half and place in 3-quart pitcher or punch bowl. Pour hot punch over sliced fruit. Serve piping hot in mugs and garnish with one each of the orange and lemon half-cartwheels.

Makes 8 cups.

Hot Mulled Wine
6 to 8 minutes

1 qt. red wine
1 cinnamon stick
3 whole cloves
6 whole
   peppercorns
Rind of one whole
   lemon, thinly
   peeled

Combine ingredients in 1½-quart mixing bowl. Heat 6 to 8 minutes. Pour into cups or mugs and serve hot.

Makes 1 quart.

Lemonade Hot Toddy
7 to 9 minutes

1 can (12 oz.) frozen
  lemonade
  concentrate,
  thawed and
  undiluted
Water
Bourbon

Open thawed lemonade, stir to blend. Pour 4 ounces of water into each of six 8-ounce mugs. Heat 7 to 9 minutes. Add to each mug 4 tablespoons (2 ounces) lemonade concentrate and 3 tablespoons (1½ ounces) bourbon. Stir and serve.

Makes 6 servings.

Discotheque Diablo
10 to 12 minutes

1 cup firmly packed
  brown sugar
1 cup creamy
  peanut butter
6 cups freshly
  made coffee
1 cup whipping
  cream

In a 2-quart mixing bowl, cream brown sugar and peanut butter until thoroughly blended. Add coffee slowly, stirring constantly, until sugar and peanut butter mixture dissolves. Pour coffee mixture into mugs. Heat 10 to 12 minutes, until bubbly.

While coffee mixture is heating, whip cream. Put an equal amount in each mug. Pour hot coffee mixture over cream. Serve at once.

Makes 6 servings.

Hot Mulled Wine

Index